NEW DIRECTIONS FOR INSTITUTIONAL RESEARCH

# Organizing Effective Institutional Research Offices

Jennifer B. Presley
*EDITOR*

NUMBER 66, SUMMER 1990
JOSSEY-BASS INC., PUBLISHERS

Gutman

NEW DIRECTIONS FOR INSTITUTIONAL RESEARCH



# Organizing Effective Institutional Research Offices

Jennifer B. Presley
*University of Massachusetts at Boston*

*EDITOR*

Number 66, Summer 1990

JOSSEY-BASS INC., PUBLISHERS
San Francisco • Oxford

Organizing Effective Institutional Research Offices.
*Jennifer B. Presley* (ed.).
New Directions for Institutional Research, no. 66.
Volume XVII, Number 2.





NEW DIRECTIONS FOR INSTITUTIONAL RESEARCH is part of The Jossey-Bass
Higher Education Series and is published quarterly by Jossey-Bass
Inc., Publishers (publication number USPS 098-830). Second-class
postage paid at San Francisco, California, and at additional mailing
offices. Postmaster: Send address changes to Jossey-Bass Inc.,
Publishers, 350 Sansome Street, San Francisco, California 94104.

EDITORIAL CORRESPONDENCE should be sent to the Editor-in-Chief,
Patrick T. Terenzini, Center for the Study of Higher Education, 133
Willard Building, The Pennsylvania State University, University Park,
Pennsylvania 16802.



Library of Congress Catalog Card Number LC 85-645339

International Standard Serial Number ISSN 0271-0579

International Standard Book Number ISBN 1-55542-829-0



Manufactured in the United States of America. Printed on acid-free paper.

THE ASSOCIATION FOR INSTITUTIONAL RESEARCH was created in 1966 to benefit, assist, and advance research leading to improved understanding, planning, and operation of institutions of higher education. Publication policy is set by its Publications Board.



For information about the Association for Institutional Research, write to:

AIR Executive Office
314 Stone Building
Florida State University
Tallahassee, FL 32306-3038

(904) 644-4470

# CONTENTS

# EDITOR'S NOTES

Five years ago, on the occasion of the twenty-fifth annual forum of the Association for Institutional Research, Peterson and Corcoran edited a volume of New Directions for Institutional Research (number 46, June 1985) entitled *Institutional Research in Transition.* Its central purpose was to provide a prospective view of where institutional research was heading as a profession. Peterson concluded that institutional research was in a period of "fragmentation and uncertainty" (Peterson and Corcoran, 1985, p. 12), spurred on by the challenges of several conditions—the development of planning and policy analysis as an entity separate from institutional research, the tendency of individual units to engage in research as a defense against retrenchment, and the advent of microcomputers. Subsequent experience suggests that these conditions, coupled with the increased political currency of institutional accountability and assessment, are in fact leading to a different conclusion about the state of institutional research as we reach the end of the decade.

The number of institutions engaging in institutional research appears to be growing, spurred on by these external trends. For many institutional researchers who are establishing an analytical capacity for the first time, the challenges come not from the competition of other analysts within an organization who have the tools and skills to undertake their own institutional research, but from a lack of centralized management of data or of structures to support an analytical approach to decision making. These institutional researchers are usually charged with *centralizing* reporting for the first time, not with managing the decentralization of an already established structure. Only a few institutions have evolved to a level of analytical sophistication and data management manifested by decentralization, or fragmentation, to use Peterson's terminology.

The growing strength of institutional research as a professional enterprise is demonstrated by the growth in membership in the Association for Institutional Research (AIR) which has increased by 500, or almost 40 percent, since 1984. And there is plenty of room for continued expansion. While over a thousand U.S. institutions are represented through AIR membership, this still represents only one-third of all U.S. institutions of higher education. Of the twenty-nine public institutions in Massachusetts, for example, fewer than ten have any significant institutional research capacity. Among those that do, most have developed within the last five years. Even within the institutions represented through AIR membership, many have yet to take full advantage of the technical advances of the past decade or to build an analytical capacity that stands ready to support the institution in the demanding decade of the 1990s.

Major external trends are propelling institutions to become more fully involved with institutional research. Among these trends are the growth of statewide coordination of institutions and the concomitant demand for data, the changing requirements for accreditation to include an emphasis on assessment, and increasing competition between institutions, requiring a strategic (and quantitatively supported) approach to institutional management. Institutions can no longer move, with little self-knowledge, blindly into the future.

This set of circumstances leads me to propose that the development of institutional research can be viewed not as that of a single organism that began its life in the 1950s, developed rapidly during the 1960s (Doi, 1979), became institutionalized through consolidated units in the 1970s, and faced "fragmentation and uncertainty" in the 1980s (Peterson, 1985), but as a multitude of organisms (individual offices) that together constitute a complex system. Each organism has its own pace of development and limit to its ultimate sophistication.

The major mission of many offices of institutional research will always be to provide basic descriptive analyses essential to institutional self-knowledge. They are one-person offices, unlikely to grow over time into the ten-person (or more) units or decentralized networks of analysts that exist in a few large and complex institutions. This view of the developmental process has an incremental aspect to it. Offices that reach the most complex stages of maturity still depend on the elemental building blocks of institutional research—good data and flexible reporting. They must continue to satisfy these lower-order needs if they are to survive. J. Fredericks Volkwein, in the first chapter of this volume, echoes this view with his ecological model of institutional research. In this context, the "fragmentation and uncertainty" observed by Peterson (1985) applies largely to the most evolved of institutional research operations—those that in Volkwein's terminology (Chapter One) are experiencing "elaborate profusion."

## An Overview

This volume is designed to assist both those who are establishing an institutional research function for the first time and those who are invigorating an existing unit. The authors write from their own experiences as institutional researchers who have been involved with development activities. They provide guidelines for how to approach tasks and avoid major pitfalls. Seasoned institutional researchers will find that many of the chapters provide a useful update on such issues as computing tools, data administration, the establishment of assessment capacity, and interpersonal communications.

Chapter One sets the context for the volume with the results of Volkwein's recently completed study of the membership of the North East

Association for Institutional Research, a regional organization affiliated with AIR. He finds that the majority of institutional research offices are located in small institutions, staffed by one person, and burdened by the demands of routine reporting. He finds the difficulty and complexity of their tasks to be correlated most highly with the size of the professional staff, not with functional location or level in the organization's hierarchy. Two-year colleges are the most likely to draw on institutional research expertise in conducting outcomes research. He concludes his chapter with a discussion of the profession as an evolving ecological system of very different organizational arrangements.

Chapters Two through Eight address the details of establishing effective institutional research offices. Alton L. Taylor (Chapter Two) provides a theoretical framework for considering where to locate the institutional research office within the organizational structure. This chapter will help decision makers ensure an appropriate fit between location, staffing, and expectations for performance.

Chapter Three provides an introduction to institutional research itself. Michael F. Middaugh uses a systems framework to describe how institutional researchers analyze the inputs, processes, and outputs of higher education. The chapter is based on the highly successful workshop that Middaugh has given for the past three years in conjunction with the annual North East Association for Institutional Research conference. Newcomers to institutional research will find this chapter particularly useful.

Chapters Four, Five, and Six form a trilogy that addresses how to access and organize institutional data for effective reporting and studies. Many institutions, not only small ones, and not only those establishing new institutional research offices, face data anarchy. Many campuses developed data-collection systems and procedures before technology enabled institutional research offices to have direct access to campus computer systems. In addition, the absence of policies for reporting "official" institutional numbers can result in institutions appearing to lack control over their operations.

Having struggled with the task of extracting research and reporting data from a variety of operational data systems both within and outside academia, Jennifer Wilton, in the first of these chapters, provides guidance to those who find themselves faced with what would only be described as "chaos" with regard to their institutional data. In Chapter Five, Karen L. Miselis outlines the data-administration approach to dealing with data anarchy. She draws on her experience with the University of Pennsylvania, one of the leaders in higher education in establishing new structures and procedures for managing information resources and administering data. Miselis describes how to begin incorporating this new aspect of the management enterprise into an organization's culture. New and ever-changing computing technology has been a major impetus toward giving renewed importance to institutional research and to the concomitant need for effective data administration. Institutional researchers must not only ensure the quality and timeliness of institutional data but also marshal the technological resources that will enable them to operate effectively. In Chapter Six, William L. Tetlow describes some strategies he has found useful in assisting a variety of institutions to establish or update the computing capacity of their institutional research offices.

In Chapter Seven, James O. Nichols and Lori A. Wolff address how to organize for effective assessment. The University of Mississippi, as a member of the Southern Association of Colleges and Schools regional accrediting association, has had early experience with the growing importance of assessment to the accreditation process. Nichols and Wolff summarize the assessment movement of the 1980s and provide concrete advice for establishing an assessment capacity on campus. Their guidelines and remarks will be useful both to the newcomer and to the seasoned institutional researcher whose scope of responsibility has expanded to incorporate this activity.

The ultimate reward for our labor is knowing that our work makes a difference. Chapter Eight provides some important precepts for effective action. Institutional research that is undertaken without due consideration for the needs and culture of the organization of which it is a part is doomed to disuse, if not uselessness. Felice D. Billups and Lenore A. DeLucia remind us of the institutional researcher's role as activist and communicator. They lay out some tenets for good communication practice that will help to ensure that the work of the institutional researcher is not disregarded. We would all be well served if we reviewed these guidelines each year, for none of us is immune from allowing our small piece of the universe to take on inappropriate importance in our minds.

In the final chapter, I summarize the major themes of the chapters and discuss the authors' recommendations in terms of my own experience in building an effective institutional research office.

Jennifer B. Presley
Editor

## References

Doi, J. I. "The Beginnings of a Profession." In R. G. Cope (ed.), *Professional Development for Institutional Research: A Retrospective View.* New Directions for Institutional Research, no. 23. San Francisco: Jossey-Bass, 1979.

Peterson, M. W. "Institutional Research: An Evolutionary Perspective." In M. W. Peterson and M. Corcoran (eds.), *Institutional Research in Transition.* New Directions for Institutional Research, no. 46. San Francisco: Jossey-Bass, 1985.

*Jennifer B. Presley is executive director of the office of policy research and planning at the University of Massachusetts at Boston. She is president of the North East Association for Institutional Research (1989–1990).*

*This chapter brings data to bear on four current issues in institutional research: professional role identity, location in the organizational hierarchy, proliferation of functions and tasks, and support for assessment. The conclusion describes four different types of institutional research offices.*

# The Diversity of Institutional Research Structures and Tasks

*J. Fredericks Volkwein*

In their studies of higher education, sociologists have examined the conflict between the faculty's *institutional* role (to provide instruction for students) and the faculty's *professional* role (to carry out research and scholarship). For example, Caplow and McGee (1958) noted that many institutions hire faculty to teach but give them promotions and professional visibility for their research and scholarship.

Institutional researchers, while not facing exactly the same dilemma, may nevertheless find a dichotomy between the routine tasks their institutions require of them and the kinds of analyses they find personally and professionally rewarding. Because of the heavy demands made on them for routine reporting to internal and external audiences (their institutional role), some institutional researchers find little time to conduct the challenging, problem-focused analyses that drew them to the field and for which they received their graduate training (their professional role).

This role dichotomy is complicated by the incomplete evolution of institutional research as a distinct profession. Peterson (1985) described the evolution of the profession over the past four decades and indicated that we have entered a period of fragmentation and uncertainty. The professional and organizational literature suggests that professionals attain higher status, at least in part, by higher levels of education and experience (Etzioni, 1984; Hall, 1988). The more that institutional research offices are

The author is deeply indebted to three people at The State University of New York at Albany who assisted with the data analysis: graduate students Yong Soon Im and Diane Hannahs and assistant for institutional research Marios Agrotes.

staffed by full-time professionals who earn advanced degrees and remain in their careers for a good many years, the greater the claim we can make for institutional research as a distinct profession. More importantly, years of experience and levels of education are assumed to have a bearing on the nature of the tasks performed. Higher levels of training and experience should be associated with higher-level tasks. The ambiguity of professional identity is the first of four major issues confronting institutional research as a field of practice.

A second concern is the extent to which institutional research activities should be organizationally centralized or decentralized. Peterson and Corcoran (1985) expressed concern about the emergence of research activities in a wide range of other campus offices. This "proliferation" of institutional research throughout the campus is receiving attention in the recent literature. Hearn and Corcoran (1988) explored the factors behind the emergence of research activities in noncentral units, postulated three theoretical arguments to explain such proliferation, and found support for their theories in a case study of the University of Minnesota. Schmidtlein (1985) has warned about the potential dangers of such dispersion, including redundancy, unnecessary competition, and loss of some advantages of scale. But Hearns and Corcoran not only explained some of the general forces working to promote proliferation but also noted several organizational benefits to be derived therefrom.

A third, related set of issues pertains to the appropriate location of institutional research functions and offices in the organizational structure. Organizational structures and the people who occupy them place both demands and constraints on the labor performed. Thus, the work of an office is influenced by its location in the organizational hierarchy as well as by the expertise of its staff. The office's research agenda is shaped by the host office, which in turn receives power from the information generated by institutional research (Schmidtlein, 1985).

The literature contains several conceptual frameworks useful to understanding institutional research functions. A systems view sees organizations as a variety of subsystems interacting with each other and with the organization's environment. For example, Katz and Kahn (1978) describe the managerial or executive subsystem (headed by a college president or chancellor), the production subsystem (the academic structure that produces teaching and research), the maintenance-and-support subsystem (accounting, budgeting, payroll, housing, dining, personnel, buildings and grounds, and similar support services), adaptive subsystems (for example, planning, analysis, and environmental scanning), and boundary subsystems (such as admissions and public relations).

A second useful framework is described by Mintzberg (1979), who identifies five basic parts of all organizations: (1) the Strategic Apex (similar to Katz and Kahn's managerial subsystem), (2) the Operating Core (similar to Katz and Kahn's production subsystem), (3) the Middle Line (consisting of vice presidents, deans, and heads of large divisions), (4) the Support Staff (similar to Katz and Kahn's support subsystem), and (5) the Technostructure (similar to Katz and Kahn's adaptive subsystem).

Taylor (1989) applied just such a framework to a study of twenty-seven institutional research offices and found widely variable structures and tasks based on organizational location. He further explores this framework in Chapter Two.

A fourth issue involves the extent to which institutional research offices are or should be involved in assessing student outcomes and institutional effectiveness. A 1987 survey of 167 campuses in the Southern Regional Accrediting Association found that few institutions were actively responding to the need to demonstrate their educational effectiveness and to provide evidence about student outcomes (Rogers and Gentemann, 1989). A minority of the institutional research offices in the study reported that they conducted outcomes research and supported program-evaluation studies. Ory and Parker (1989), in a telephone survey conducted in the fall of 1988, found that very few large research universities assess learning outcomes or gains in student achievement.

Most colleges and universities are under pressure from accrediting bodies, trustees, parents, and state officials to demonstrate their educational effectiveness. Offices of institutional research represent one of the few sources of administrative research expertise, yet most institutional research offices do not provide such information and support, or are unable to do so (Rogers and Gentemann, 1989).

Thus, four overlapping subjects of conflict or discussion are now emerging in the field of institutional research: professional-role identity, location in the organizational hierarchy, proliferation of functions and tasks, and support for assessment.

The results of a recent survey provide a perspective on these subjects (Volkwein, Agrotes, and Hannahs, 1989). We sent surveys to 198 North East Association for Institutional Research (NEAIR) member institutions in April 1989 and received responses from 141 campuses. This survey collected information about the staff size, educational preparation, and years of experience of those carrying out administrative research and analysis functions. We also requested information about the location of these offices and the title of the person to whom the office reports. Finally, we listed over three dozen functional tasks and asked respondents to indicate the degree to which these various internal analyses, external reporting activities, and special studies are centralized versus the degree to which they are decentralized at their campuses. We categorized institutions according to size (student enrollment) and Carnegie Classification. More specific information about the methodology is available in our conference paper (Volkwein, Agrotes, and Hannahs, 1989).

## Professional Identity

If common nomenclatures, advanced degrees, similar training, and common tasks are necessary for professional identity, the field of institutional research is still maturing. Two-thirds of the offices use titles like "institutional research," "institutional studies," or "institutional analysis." In some of the remaining cases, especially some smaller schools, "institutional research" is paired with another functional title, such as planning, information management, records, or grants. However, institutional research functions and tasks also use a variety of other rubrics such as information management and policy analysis, financial planning and analytical studies, planning and evaluation, enrollment research, and planning and enrollment management, among others.

Barely half of the NEAIR professionals work in offices of three or more headed by a person possessing a doctorate. Figure 1 shows the staffing levels of the responding offices. Only twenty-nine of 141 campuses have professional work groups of three or more. Sixty-four of these offices have only one full-time professional. Twenty-five of the campuses have only part-time institutional research staff, and nineteen of these have no formal organizational structure called institutional research (or its equivalent) and no professional staff person with a related job title. Thus, most of our

**Figure 1. Professional Staff in Offices of Institutional Research at 141 NEAIR Campuses**

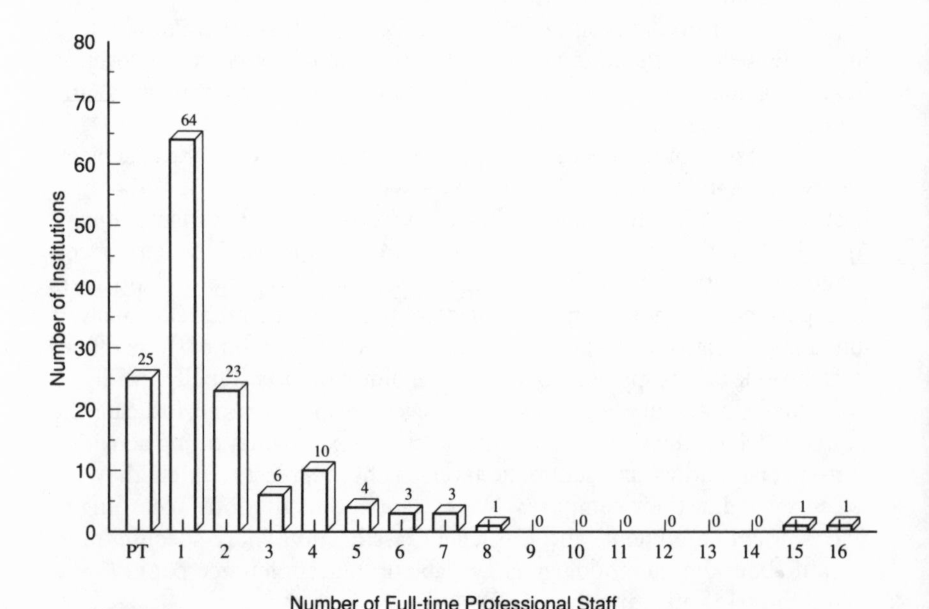

analysis concentrates on the 122 campuses reporting a formal institutional research structure.

Table 1 shows the profile of the 265 full-time professional staff in the 122 institutions with identifiable institutional research units. About 79 percent hold at least a masters degree, but only one in three has completed a doctorate. Only 52 percent of the responding offices are headed by a person with a doctoral degree. Regarding their fields of educational training, 39 percent received their most recent degree in the social sciences and 26 percent in education; mathematics and science (including engineering and computer science) account for 14 percent, and business fields 11 percent. This suggests that institutional research professionals possess quite diverse backgrounds, training, and experience.

About one-fourth of the professionals are veterans with over ten years of experience, while another one-fourth are newcomers with two years or less. The institutional research profession, therefore, can be characterized by a good deal of mobility, and only a quarter of the current professional staff have been in the field long enough to be making an apparent career commitment.

A significant relationship between staff size, educational level, and years of experience is shown in Table 2. Nearly all large offices have one or more doctorate holders on the staff as well as staff with several years of experience. The majority of those in the smallest offices do not hold a doctoral degree, and many are relative newcomers to the field. This suggests that an informal professional hierarchy may be evolving, analogous to that which exists in many academic fields and significantly associated with department size.

**Table 1. Description of Staff in Institutional Research Offices**

| | |
|---|---|
| *Highest Degree* | |
| Doctorate | 33% |
| Master's | 46% |
| *Academic Field of Highest Degree* | |
| Social Science | 39% |
| Education | 26% |
| Mathematics and Science | 14% |
| Business | 11% |
| Humanities | 8% |
| *Years of Experience in Institutional Research* | |
| 0–2 | 27% |
| 3–5 | 27% |
| 6–10 | 21% |
| 11 or more | 25% |

*Note:* Table profiles 265 staff members in 122 institutions.

*Source:* Volkwein, Agrotes, and Hannahs, 1989.

**Table 2. The Size of the Professional Staff in Relation to the Highest Degree and Years of Experience ($N = 122$)**

| | *Professional Staff Size* | | | | | | | | |
|---|---|---|---|---|---|---|---|---|---|
| | *Less than Two* | | | *Two or Three* | | | *Four or More* | | |
| *Greatest Number of Years of Experience on IR Staff* | *0–3* | *4–10* | *11+* | *0–3* | *4–10* | *11+* | *0–3* | *4–10* | *11+* |
| Highest degree on IR staff | | | | | | | | | |
| Bachelor's | 4 | 2 | 0 | 0 | 0 | 0 | 0 | 0 | 0 |
| Master's | 14 | 14 | 7 | 3 | 5 | 4 | 0 | 1 | 2 |
| Doctorate | 4 | 14 | 11 | 2 | 10 | 6 | 0 | 3 | 16 |
| Total | 22 | 30 | 18 | 5 | 15 | 10 | 0 | 4 | 18 |

## Organizational Location

Table 3 shows the organizational arrangement for institutional research offices by campus size. *Administrative location* refers to the functional location of the institutional research unit within the organizational structure. The institutional research unit most often (fifty-six campuses) is lodged in the executive, or managerial, subsystem, headed by the campus chief executive officer, especially in smaller colleges. The second most common pattern (thirty-five campuses) places the institutional research unit in the production structure, in academic affairs. On the remaining campuses, the institutional research unit is located in the various support and adaptive subsystems, especially planning and budgeting.

*Organizational level* refers to the level of the director's supervisor. At smaller campuses the institutional research office tends to report to the chief executive, although in some cases the function is part of the duties of an assistant to the president or registrar. As institutions increase in size, institutional research directors are most likely to report to a vice president. Interestingly, colleges with enrollments between 2,500 and 5,000 are most likely to place institutional research at organizational levels below vice president. Twenty-one of the thirty campuses that place institutional research at the lower administrative levels are two-year institutions (eleven) or comprehensive colleges (ten). In the largest doctoral institutions, institutional research is most often placed under a vice president for academic affairs, planning, or financial management.

Based on the literature, we expected to find larger, more professionally trained staffs in larger, more diverse educational organizations. This is true, as shown in Table 4. The size of the institutional research staff is highly correlated with campus size (.73) and with the Carnegie Classification (.60). These in turn are significantly correlated with years of experience and highest degree on the staff. However, we found little significant correlation between the other professional variables and the location of the institutional research unit within the organization. Large doctorate-granting institutions are more likely to have offices with four or more professional staff, at least one of whom possesses an earned doctorate and many years of experience.

## Task Variables

Table 5 lists in descending order the three dozen tasks we asked respondents to rate on a scale from centralized to decentralized. The first column shows the percent of campuses that centralize these functions in an institutional research unit. The second column shows the percent of tasks shared between the institutional research office and another office.

More than 75 percent of respondents play a significant role in the

**Table 3. Organizational Locations of Institutional Research Offices by Campus Size (*N* = 141)**

| | *Administrative Location of Institutional Research Function* | | | | | | | |
|---|---|---|---|---|---|---|---|---|
| | *Executive Apex (N = 56)* | | | *Production Subsystem (Academic Affairs) (N = 35)* | | *Support and Adaptive Subsystems (All Other Admin. Divis./Areas) (N = 31)* | | *No Identifiable IR Office* |
| *Administrative Title IR Is Responsible to:* | *President or CEO* | *Vice-Pres. (or equiv.)* | *Below Vice-Pres.* | *Vice-Pres. (or equiv.)* | *Below Vice-Pres.* | *Vice-Pres. (or equiv.)* | *Below Vice-Pres.* | *Dispersed* |
| *Size (FTE Students):* | | | | | | | | |
| Under 2,500 | 20 | 3 | 2 | 5 | 2 | 5 | 2 | 14 |
| 2,500–4,999 | 6 | 2 | 4 | 6 | 7 | 5 | 2 | 4 |
| 5,000–9,999 | 10 | 2 | 2 | 5 | 2 | 7 | 3 | 0 |
| 10,000+ | 2 | 2 | 1 | 7 | 1 | 5 | 2 | 1 |
| Total | 38 | 9 | 9 | 23 | 12 | 22 | 9 | 19 |

**Table 4. Correlations Between the Organizational and Professional Variables Used in this Study (N = 122)**

| | *Professional Variables* | | |
|---|---|---|---|
| *Organizational Variables* | *Staff Size* | *Years of Experience* | *Highest Degree* |
| Campus size | .73 | .37 | .45 |
| Carnegie Classification | .60 | .38 | .39 |
| Functional location of institutional research | .22 | ns | ns |
| Level of institutional research in hierarchy | ns | ns | ns |

first dozen tasks. Ranking especially high in the centralized column are student attrition/retention studies, enrollment reporting, reporting of student characteristics, responding to surveys and external requests for data, and producing fact-book information. The questionnaire responses indicate that these tasks are usually centralized in an institutional research office or in one other office and are decentralized on very few campuses.

On the other end of the scale, institutional researchers overall are seldom, or only peripherally, involved in preparing campus budget requests, producing research and resource development statistics, projecting revenue, reviewing academic programs, collecting student ratings of instruction, and developing campus databases and information systems. These activities in general appear to be carried out by other offices, sometimes in cooperation with institutional researchers.

Next, we examined the data for evidence of a relationship between tasks and organizational location. We identified the tasks that most closely support the campuswide executive function, academic affairs (teaching and research), and the various support functions, such as planning and finance. Since the vast majority of institutional research offices (75 percent) are housed in the president's and academic affairs divisions, we gave particular attention to the tasks judged to be most congruent with those two functions.

We found surprisingly little relationship between organizational and task variables. Regardless of campus size, institution type, and organizational reporting relationships, institutional research offices are equally likely to participate in such specialized activities as environmental scanning, enrollment projections, and faculty workload analyses. Moreover, they are equally *unlikely* to participate in revenue projections, space-allocation studies, and student ratings of instruction. Among the three dozen task variables, responses differed in only a handful of cases, sometimes in counterintuitive ways:

**Table 5. Most Frequent Tasks Carried Out by NEAIR Member Institutions (*N* = 122)**

| | *Percentage of Campus Responses* | | |
|---|---|---|---|
| | *Centralized in Inst. Res.* | *Shared* | *Total* |
| Enrollment management studies | | | |
| Attrition/retention-related | 66 | 27 | 93 |
| Admissions-related | 27 | 55 | 82 |
| Reporting enrollment data | 52 | 34 | 86 |
| Reporting other student characteristics (for example, race, gender, geographical origin) | 57 | 29 | 86 |
| Supplying national survey data | 67 | 18 | 85 |
| Granting requests for data exchange | 71 | 11 | 82 |
| College guidebook surveys | 58 | 23 | 81 |
| State-related requests for data | 60 | 21 | 81 |
| Enrollment projections | 47 | 33 | 80 |
| Producing campus fact book | 66 | 11 | 77 |
| Faculty workload analyses | 49 | 27 | 76 |
| Degrees-awarded statistics | 49 | 27 | 76 |
| Studies of student academic performance | 37 | 32 | 69 |
| Research on campuswide issues | 48 | 20 | 68 |
| Student opinion surveys | 45 | 23 | 68 |
| Environmental scanning | 43 | 24 | 67 |
| Salary studies | 33 | 31 | 64 |
| Generating personnel statistics | 12 | 48 | 60 |
| Alumni studies | 29 | 31 | 60 |
| Reporting admissions quality indicators | 16 | 42 | 58 |
| Assessment of student outcomes | | | 49 |
| Measurement of general educational and intellectual growth | 10 | 21 | 31 |
| Measurement of personal/social/non-cognitive student growth | 10 | 17 | 27 |
| Measurement of achievement in the academic major | 8 | 18 | 26 |
| Measurement of students' basic skills | 4 | 18 | 22 |
| Accreditation related studies | 21 | 27 | 48 |
| Preparing the campus planning document | 26 | 22 | 48 |
| Economic impact studies | 27 | 20 | 47 |
| Budget/cost/resource allocation analysis | 9 | 35 | 44 |
| Affirmative action compliance data | 15 | 28 | 43 |
| Space-allocation statistics and analysis | 15 | 26 | 41 |
| Academic program reviews | 6 | 27 | 33 |
| Revenue projections | 4 | 28 | 32 |
| Statistics on students' ratings of instruction | 20 | 9 | 29 |
| Research funding trends | 9 | 16 | 25 |
| Resource development statistics | 3 | 13 | 16 |
| Preparing campus budget request | 3 | 12 | 15 |
| Development of databases and information systems | 6 | 6 | 12 |

• Institutional research offices located in academic affairs divisions are least likely to be involved in academic program reviews. (Offices are most likely to participate in academic-program reviews when located in community colleges and reporting to the president.)

• Budget and resource-allocation studies are performed least commonly in institutional research offices reporting to the academic-affairs division, regardless of institution type.

• Institutional research responsibility for gathering and reporting affirmative action compliance data is least common when institutional research is located in the academic-affairs division and most common when it is located in one of the nonpresidential support units.

• Conducting student-opinion surveys is most likely to be centralized in the institutional research office at two-year colleges and decentralized at doctoral universities.

• Analyses of enrollments and student characteristics tend to be centralized, except at liberal arts colleges where the institutional research office shares the responsibility with others.

• Faculty-workload and -salary studies are most often centralized in the institutional research office at doctoral universities, regardless of organizational location.

As shown in Table 5, a core of tasks are carried out by most respondents, regardless of campus type and location in the administrative hierarchy. While those in the executive subsystem report slightly more involvement in executive and campuswide tasks, the results are not statistically significant. Similarly, those in the other administrative divisions report slightly more frequent responsibility for tasks in their functional areas, such as academic affairs, business and finance, and planning, but the differences are trivial until one looks at their research initiatives rather than at their routine tasks. The special studies category appears most often to reveal the organizational location of the institutional research office. Most such offices carry out a set of common activities, but their special ad hoc research activities are shaped by the host office.

Because of the foregoing, we were especially interested in the nature of special initiatives conducted by respondents. Table 6 shows the number of campuses reporting responsibility for various categories of special studies. The respondents indicated a high degree of involvement in studies related to student attrition and retention, academic performance, and student-opinion surveys. Other frequently named studies—in admissions, alumni, outcomes, and accreditation—are usually conducted in partnership with at least one other office.

## Hierarchy of Tasks

As part of our analysis, we made judgments about the difficulty and complexity of each task. For example, the degree of training and expertise

**Table 6. Special Initiatives and Studies Reported by NEAIR Member Institutions ($N$ = 122)**

| *Type of Initiatives and Studies* | *No. Campuses* |
|---|---|
| Attrition/retention | 112 |
| Admissions/enrollment management[a] | 99 |
| Student academic performance | 84 |
| Student-opinion surveys | 83 |
| Alumni studies[a] | 71 |
| Assessment of educational outcomes[a] | 60 |
| Accreditation-related studies[a] | 58 |
| Academic program reviews[a] | 40 |
| Miscellaneous academic issues | 31 |
| Miscellaneous finance and budget issues | 27 |
| Miscellaneous campus issues (for example, child care) | 29 |
| Miscellaneous student affairs issues | 19 |
| Information systems/technology/computing[a] | 14 |

[a]In the majority of cases, these initiatives were reportedly conducted in partnership with at least one other office.

required to report enrollment numbers was judged to be at a lower level than making enrollment projections, and conducting enrollment management studies requires still greater expertise. Similarly, all tasks were rated as high, medium, or low in difficulty and complexity. In general, special studies, assessment, survey research, and other work requiring expertise in research methods and statistics rated highest. Traditional institutional research reporting activities such as responding to surveys, producing a fact book, and reporting student characteristics rated lowest.

Based on the organizational and professional literature, we expected to find that this task hierarchy is related both to organizational and to professional variables. Are larger research offices and more highly trained, experienced staffs more likely to carry out higher-level responsibilities?

The results are shown by the zero-order correlations and regression beta weights in Table 7. In the first column, the task hierarchy is most significantly correlated with the size of the professional staff, followed by years of experience, highest degree, and campus size. The functional location of the institutional research unit and its level in the hierarchy are unrelated to the task hierarchy. The results support our expectation that larger staffs with higher scores on the professional variables (such as level of training and years of experience) perform more complex tasks. As expected, the correlations with institutional size and Carnegie Classification are also significant, in part due to their correlations with the professional variables shown in Table 4. But the organizational variables, especially hierarchical location, appear to have less influence on the difficulty and complexity of tasks carried out by offices than do the professional variables. This is seen even more dramatically in the second column of Table 7,

**Table 7. Regression Beta Weights and Correlations for Task Hierarchy with the Professional and Organizational Variables**

| | *Zero Order Correlations* | *Regression Beta Weights* |
|---|---|---|
| Professional staff size | .41[a] | .41[b] |
| Years of experience | .31[a] | .16 |
| Highest degree earned | .25[b] | .11 |
| FTE enrollment | .27[b] | .07 |
| Carnegie Classification | .22[c] | .07 |
| Administrative location: level | .00 | .05 |
| Administrative location: function | .02 | .08 |
| | | $R^2$ = .20[a] |

[a] .001 level
[b] .01 level
[c] .05 level

which shows the regression beta weights using task hierarchy as the dependent variable. The number of full-time professionals is the only variable to achieve statistical significance. Its influence is so strongly associated with the task hierarchy that it overwhelms the effects of the other variables in accounting for 20 percent of the explained variance.

However, task hierarchy is not as predictable from institutional characteristics as we expected. For example, we studied the twenty-five (out of 122) institutions scoring highest on the task hierarchy, led by the University of Delaware. Some of these twenty-five have well-staffed institutional research offices, but at least half do not. Evidently, a large number of one- and two-person offices are carrying out enrollment-management analyses, outcomes assessment, and other kinds of research studies, just like the larger offices.

Reviewing the twenty-nine campuses that have three or more institutional research professional staff gives another perspective. First, no small institutions appear on this list (only two have enrollments under 5,000, for example, and none under 4,000). Second, twenty-five of the twenty-nine rank in the top half in terms of years of experience and advanced degrees held by staff (led by the University of Connecticut, American University, the University of Delaware, and Georgetown University). Third, all but four of these twenty-nine rank in the top half of the task hierarchy. Hence, the size of the professional staff is linked to the size of the institution and is the most important influence on the nature of the staff and its tasks.

## Assessment

To collect information about the extent of involvement in organized assessment on each campus by the institutional research office, we used a framework borrowed in part from Jacobi, Astin, and Ayala (1987), and in part from the State University of New York (Burke, 1988). Assessment is divided into four categories: basic skills, general education, attainment in the major, and personal and social growth. Table 8 shows for each category of assessment the proportion of campuses reporting no assessment activity, assessment with a role given to the institutional research office, assessment located in another office, or assessment that is decentralized or dispersed. The results indicate that basic-skills assessment is the most common, being conducted on 82 percent of the NEAIR campuses and by 100 percent of the two-year colleges. Even among doctoral campuses, only 37 percent report no basic-skills assessment.

Measuring the noncognitive personal and social growth of students is the least common assessment activity. Forty percent of the respondents and 52 percent of the doctoral institutions indicate no assessment of personal and social growth.

We examined the assessment responses for differences according to institution type and organizational location of the institutional research unit. Organizational location made no difference in the response patterns, but we found an interesting contrast between the two-year and doctoral campuses. In three of the four types of assessment (basic skills, general education, and personal and social development), doctoral institutions reported the least activity. In contrast, two-year colleges reported the most assessment in two categories (basic skills and general education) and in every one of the four categories the most involvement by their institutional research offices. Apparently, two-year colleges are the most likely to draw on institutional research expertise in conducting outcomes research. However, even at large research universities, we found more outcomes assessment than Ory and Parker did in their telephone survey (1989).

However, the role of most respondents in these assessment efforts is not great. Offices report least involvement in basic-skills assessment (22 percent), the most common assessment activity. They participate most in assessment of students' general education and intellectual growth, yet less than one-third are so involved. Nor is there much evidence for a highly decentralized or dispersed pattern of organized assessment activities. As expected, the most decentralized assessment is in the major (31 percent), and the least decentralized is in general education (19 percent). Overall, slightly less than half the offices are engaged in some type of outcomes research (see Table 5), which is consistent with the Rogers and Gentemann study of 167 institutions in the South (1989).

Taken as a whole, the data in Table 8 suggest that approaches to assessment are highly campus-specific. Except for the universal presence of basic-skills assessment on two-year campuses, and the generally lower participation in assessment of all types by doctoral institutions, little pattern appears in the responses. On some campuses, these activities are highly

## Table 8. Assessment Activities in NEAIR Institutions

| Type of Assessment | Locus of Assessment | Percentage for All Institutions | Range of Percents by Type of Institution | |
|---|---|---|---|---|
| | | | Lowest | Highest |
| Basic skills | No assessment | 18 | Two-year = 0 | Doctoral = 37 |
| | IR role | 22 | Doctoral and comprehensive = 13 | Two-year = 40 |
| | One other office | 34 | Doctoral = 20 | Two-year = 47 |
| | Decentralized | 26 | Two-year = 13 | Comprehensive = 35 |
| General education | No assessment | 36 | Two-year = 30 | Doctoral = 43 |
| | IR role | 31 | Liberal arts = 19 | Two-year = 47 |
| | One other office | 15 | Two-year = 13 | Liberal arts = 24 |
| | Decentralized | 19 | Two-year = 10 | Comprehensive = 30 |
| Attainment in major | No assessment | 31 | Comprehensive = 22 | Two-year = 37 |
| | IR role | 26 | Liberal arts = 13 | Two-year = 39 |
| | One other office | 12 | Two-year = 7 | Liberal arts = 27 |
| | Decentralized | 31 | Two-year = 17 | Comprehensive = 48 |
| Personal/social | No assessment | 40 | Liberal arts = 25 | Doctoral = 52 |
| | IR role | 27 | Comprehensive = 22 | Two-year and comprehensive = 33 |
| | One other office | 12 | Comprehensive = 5 | Liberal arts = 29 |
| | Decentralized | 21 | Two-year = 10 | Comprehensive = 38 |

centralized, while on campuses of a similar type they are highly dispersed or even nonexistent.

## Conclusion

Our study of structures and tasks at 122 NEAIR campuses produced a few findings that are consistent with our expectations and the organizational literature. Larger research offices are generally found at larger institutions ranking higher on the Carnegie Classification. Larger offices tend to have more highly trained and experienced staffs, and they tend to carry out a more complex array of tasks. While these relationships are in the expected direction and are statistically significant, they are not nearly strong enough to predict the situation at individual campuses with any degree of certainty. Lack of predictive power is due to the wide diversity of organizational arrangements and tasks. While a cluster of tasks is common to most institutional research offices, we also found evidence of specialization and decentralization. Moreover, the location of the institutional research unit in the administrative hierarchy is highly variable. Taken as a whole, our findings are generally congruent with the single-institution Hearn and Corcoran finding that management styles, personalities, career paths, and power arrangements influenced distinctive institutional research structures and tasks (1988).

A few characteristics of the data set probably served to reduce the variance between institutions, thereby lowering the correlation coefficients. For example, only eight large universities in the NEAIR have enrollments over 20,000, and only half a dozen others have a full-time equivalent enrollment over 15,000. The relative absence of large research institutions no doubt reduced the variability of the responses. Another factor that reduces variance is the cluster of about a dozen activities that nearly all institutional research offices perform. Whether reporting to the president or the budget officer, institutional research staff communicate facts and figures about their institutions both internally and externally and are heavily involved in various kinds of enrollment management studies.

Another explanation for the weak correlation relates to outcomes assessment. The task hierarchy gave a high score to assessment and educational outcomes studies, which are more often undertaken by smaller institutions and community colleges. In all institutions, a portion of assessment activities is decentralized, without heavy involvement by an institutional research unit. Thus, lack of institutional research leadership in assessment also led to reduced variability. We were disappointed to find so little respondent participation in outcomes research; but given the paucity of staff in most offices, we are not surprised. Most institutional research operations are simply unprepared to undertake the effort.

The limitations of the data in this study need to be recognized. We designed the data collection instrument to be uncomplicated and easily completed. While we collected a great deal of information about structures and functions, we cannot claim to have a complete picture of the operations and activities of the various offices. Some respondents gave their answers with relative care and completeness, while others may not have taken the time to indicate their activities fully and accurately. Also, we may have failed to collect information about some professionally challenging activities that might have produced a greater spread of scores on the task hierarchy. For example, we did not seek detailed information about the technological skills of the staff nor about their involvement in developing information systems and data bases. (Some campuses supplied this in the space for additional responses.) Moreover, we are not able to gather specific information about the actual level of sophistication of the special studies that counted so heavily on the task hierarchy. We do not know which offices are simply reporting descriptive statistics and which ones are applying conceptual frameworks, building scales, and looking for data relationships.

Nevertheless, we did develop a reasonable task hierarchy and examined its relationship to several organizational and professional measures. The organizational variables appear to be unrelated to the hierarchy. Certainly, the location of the institutional research unit in the administrative structure is statistically irrelevant. While campus size and institution type are modestly correlated with the hierarchy, their influence in a regression equation is outweighed by the professional variables in general, and by staff size in particular. The size of the professional staff of the institutional research office suggests more about the nature of the work and the operation within the organization than any other single piece of information.

Viewed holistically, these data suggest that the field of institutional research, at least in the Northeast, is less a unified profession than an evolving ecology of very different organizational arrangements. We close with an overview of that ecology.

The literature on organizational life cycles identifies four stages of organizational development that parallel human development: the craft structure (infancy and childhood), small adhocracy (adolescence), professional bureaucracy (adulthood), and what we call elaborate profusion (maturity) (see Figure 2). Various authors use similar terminology, often with different meanings than those intended here, to describe the growth and evolution of entire organizations (Cameron and Whetten, 1983; Katz and Kahn, 1978; Mintzberg, 1979). These four rubrics, however, seem to capture a good deal of the diversity we observed in institutional research.

**Craft Structure.** On the majority of campuses institutional research staff consists of one person, perhaps even on a part-time basis, who is burdened by the demands of routine reporting and a modest amount of number-crunching for the institution. Analogous to childhood in human development, organizations at this stage of primitive evolution have been likened to a craft structure, where one person seeks to develop selected skills. Most of these personnel do not have doctoral degrees, although a substantial minority hold advanced degrees and appear to be building a career in institutional research. Many are current or former faculty members with doctorates in their academic disciplines, often combining institutional research with other duties. A few such offices are engaged in outcomes research and other forms of analysis. Craft structures dominate the ranks of educational institutions with enrollments under 5,000. Their members are probably most in need of support from institutional research colleagues.

**Small Adhocracy.** Proceeding clockwise around Figure 2, we find a second type, the two- or three-person office, which has grown out of childhood into a more adolescent, entrepreneurial stage. Organizations at this stage of development are characterized by a flat hierarchy, simple structure, and little specialization. The tasks of the group and the credentials of staff are varied and uneven from one campus to another. Some offices are engaged in applied-research projects, and some are not. Some are staffed by those with masters credentials, but others have doctoral degrees and more experience. Small adhocracies are responsive to their administrative hosts, account for about one-fourth of the total number of

**Figure 2. An Institutional Research Ecology**

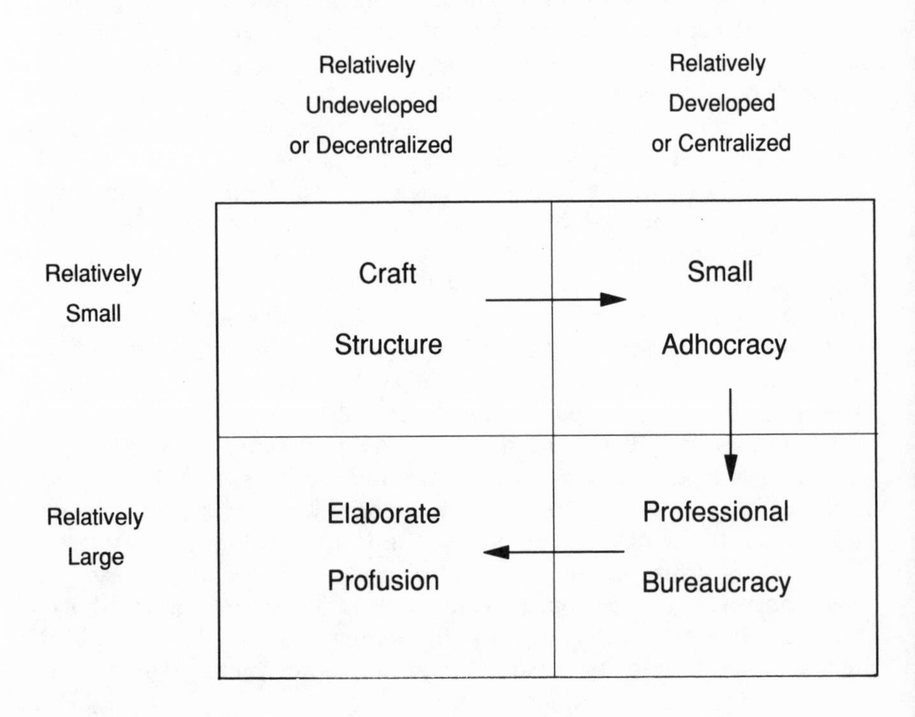

institutional research units, and tend to be found in comprehensive colleges and two-year colleges with enrollments between 5,000 and 10,000.

**Professional Bureaucracy.** The third type has achieved a level of formal organization and professional adulthood. Consisting of at least four (but usually more) professionals, these institutional research offices have developed a modest bureaucratic structure in terms of hierarchy, division of labor, and specialization. Such offices have at least one person with an earned doctorate and at least one person with ten or more years of experience. But these offices also have entry-level positions occupied by graduate assistants and others who are just getting started in the field. Such offices typically carry out a number of sophisticated research projects each year, and responsibility for these projects is more likely to be centralized in the institutional research office than on most campuses. Staff from these offices contribute actively to organizations such as AIR and NEAIR. While serving as the model for others, institutional research offices that have reached the level of professional bureaucracies constitute less than a fifth of the total, and the purest examples are found at doctoral universities such as the University of Connecticut, the University of Delaware, the University of Pittsburgh, and West Virginia University.

**Elaborate Profusion.** At the fourth stage, institutional research activities and expertise proliferate throughout the institution. On these campuses, usually research universities, the analytical environment is so complex that institutional research has become dispersed between a number of different offices reporting to different parts of the administrative hierarchy. Much institutional analysis is decentralized, if not fragmented, and only loosely coordinated. Not many institutions exhibit such elaborateness, but Boston University and Syracuse University are perhaps the leading NEAIR candidates for such classification.

Obviously, not all offices fit neatly into one of the four models, and some campuses may be in transition from one type to another. However, these descriptions do seem to capture the dominant patterns we observe in the campus responses to our survey.

The implications for the profession, of course, are enormous and deserve more attention in future studies. Institutional researchers who staff these different structures have different work environments, technical needs, and relationships with colleagues. Much of our literature has been based on studies of the developed bureaucracy, on which the professional image of institutional research is founded. However, professionals working in craft structures and those working in professional bureaucracies may feel they are employed in different occupations. The administrative arrangements and tasks for offices may be as varied as the institutions themselves. We need to ask if institutional research as a profession is adequately serving the needs of the one- and two-person offices, which constitute the majority in the Northeast, and we assume, the rest of the country. As higher education develops and as needs for information and analysis grow, it is likely that some of these smaller craft structures will become tomorrow's professional bureaucracies. The effectiveness and efficiency of the institutional research profession can only be improved by recognizing the wide diversity of structures and tasks that characterize campus practice and by designing the kind of collaborative support that is consistent with this diversity.

## References


Burke, J. C. "Campus Plans on Academic Assessment." Memorandum to Campus Presidents from the Provost of the State University of New York, December 12, 1988.

Cameron, K. S., and Whetten, D. A. Models of the Organizational Life Cycle: Applications to Higher Education. *Review of Higher Education,* 1983, *6,* 269–299.

Caplow, T., and McGee, R. J. *The Academic Marketplace.* New York: Basic Books, 1958; Anchor Books, 1965.

Etzioni, A. *Modern Organizations.* Englewood Cliffs, N.J.: Prentice-Hall, 1984.

Hall, R. H. *Organizations: Structure, Process, and Outcome.* (4th ed.) Englewood Cliffs: N.J.: Prentice-Hall, 1988.

Hearn, J. C., and Corcoran, M. E. "An Exploration of Factors Behind the Proliferation of the Institutional Research Enterprise." *Journal of Higher Education,* 1988, *59* (6), 634-651.

Jacobi, M., Astin, A., and Ayala, F., Jr. *College Student Outcomes Assessment.* ASHE-ERIC Higher Education Report, no. 7. Washington, D.C.: ERIC Clearinghouse on Higher Education and the Association for the Study of Higher Education, 1987.

Katz, D., and Kahn, R. L. *The Social Psychology of Organizations.* New York: Wiley, 1978.

Mintzberg, H. *The Structuring of Organizations.* Englewood Cliffs, N.J.: Prentice-Hall, 1979.

Ory, J. C., and Parker, S. A. "Assessment Activities at Large Research Universities." *Research in Higher Education,* 1989, *30* (4), 375-385.

Peterson, M. W., and Corcoran, M. E. (eds.). *Institutional Research in Transition.* New Directions for Institutional Research, no. 46. San Francisco: Jossey-Bass, 1985.

Rogers, B. H., and Gentemann, K. M. "The Value of IR in the Assessment of Educational Effectiveness." *Research in Higher Education,* 1989, *30* (3), 345–355.

Schmidtlein, F. "Changing Governance and Management Strategies." In M. W. Peterson and M. E. Corcoran (eds.), *Institutional Research in Transition.* New Directions for Institutional Research, no. 46. San Francisco: Jossey-Bass, 1985.

Taylor, A. L. "Organizational Structure and Institutional Research Role and Function." Paper presented at the 29th Annual Forum for Institutional Research, Baltimore, Md., April 30–May 3, 1989.

Volkwein, J. F., Agrotes, M., and Hannahs, D. "The Structure and Functions of Institutional Research Offices within NEAIR." *North East Association for Institutional Research 16th Annual Conference Proceedings,* Pittsburgh, Pa., October 21–24, 1989.


*J. Fredericks Volkwein is director of institutional research and adjunct professor of educational administration and policy studies, The State University of New York at Albany.*

*The location of the institutional research unit within the organizational structure influences the role it plays in supporting effective decision making.*

# Options for Location in the Organizational Structure

*Alton L. Taylor*

An institutional research office or unit's location within a college or university organization should fit its mission so that work may be done effectively. The logical arrangement of units varies according to factors such as individuals, tradition, size and purpose of the office, and the decision-making needs of the institution. Over the years, institutional researchers have expressed concerns about how the organizational location of their office defines their role and function. Office location has important implications for the type of work performed, the staffing needs of the office, and the influence institutional researchers have in the decision-making process of the organization. This chapter provides a conceptual framework for considering the impact of organizational location on an institutional research office.

## Background

The location of an institutional research office in the organizational structure of a college or university affects its functions and influence (Saupe, 1990). Volkwein, in Chapter One, found that while most institutional research offices carry out a set of common activities, location influences their ad hoc research activities. Other research has shown that organizational position is important to the work flow within that organization (Brass, 1984). For example, Brass, in a study of the relationships between structural positions and influence in a newspaper publishing company, reports that "access to the communication network of the dominant coalition shows significant positive relationships with the perceptual measures of influence" (p. 532) and that being in a position to control communications in an organizational unit is particularly important to the promotion process. He added that central location and accessibility to the work flow in an organization are significantly related to influence within the organization.

The institutional researcher, like the institutional research office as a whole, is influenced by organizational structure, because organizational structure imposes the ultimate constraints on the individual's potential for influence. An individual's influence in an organization depends on several factors, including the importance of his or her position in the workflow, his or her skill in coping with uncertainty, whether or not he or she occupies a boundary scanning position, and his or her network with subgroups within the organization. Because of the relationships that exist between structural position and influence in an organization, a general knowledge of the nature of organizational structures is helpful in deciding where to locate an institutional research office.

Organizational structure is defined as "the enduring characteristics of an organization reflected by the distribution of units and positions within an organization and their systematic relationships to each other" (James and Jones, 1976, p. 76). Important to designing an effective organizational structure, therefore, is the concept of division of labor. A clear definition of the organization's division indicates task positions and the interrelationships and interdependencies between positions. When work is divided into task positions, some individuals are given more power and influence than others. Accepting James and Jones' definition of organizational structure elevates the importance of where to locate and what duties to assign the institutional research office.

Mintzberg (1983) provides a conceptual framework that helps one understand organizational structure. He states that "the structure of an organization can be defined simply as the sum total of the ways in which its labor is divided into distinct tasks and then its coordination is achieved among those tasks" (p. 2). Division of labor is defined in terms of the job to be done and the technical systems required to do the job. Coordination includes those mechanisms that control and communicate the work flow throughout an organization. Mintzberg identifies five basic parts of an organization: strategic apex, middle line, operating core, technostructure, and support staff. In the following, each of these structural parts of an organization will be briefly reviewed in relation to institutions of higher education.

The *strategic apex* of a college or university includes the governing board, president, the president's staff, and executive committees. The strategic apex is composed of persons with a view of the entire organization. These persons ensure that the organization supports its mission effectively and that it meets the needs of those who have power over others working in the organization.

The *operating core* of a college or university includes members of the organization who educate students, conduct research, and provide public services. Educated graduates are the essential outputs of a college or university, and the faculty have the responsibilities for admissions, teaching, and conferring degrees to students. Thus, the members of the operating core of a college or university are primarily the faculty.

The *middle line* is located between the strategic apex and the operating core. The middle line includes persons with formal authority to monitor the work of the operating core in relation to the mission of the organization. These individuals maintain contact with analysts and support staff by monitoring the work of the operating core and formulating strategy that helps members of the operating core do their work. Middle-line managers in universities and colleges are vice-presidents, deans, and division and department chairs.

The *technostructure* is not well developed or easily noticeable in institutions of higher education. It lies outside the direct contact of the strategic apex, middle line, and operating core. In the private sector, examples of the technostructure include analysts such as industrial engineers, quality control engineers, long-range planners who assess market needs, and personnel analysts who assess the specific needs of the company and describe required personnel skills to trainers and recruiters. This part of the organization consists of analysts and planners who try to control workers by stabilizing and standardizing the work activities of the organization. Individuals in the technostructure are also concerned with an organization's adaptation to change, environmental scanning, and ways to improve organizational performance. Units in the higher education technostructure include budget offices, institutional auditors, governmental liaison offices, and public relations offices. These units are located under, but are not part of, the strategic apex or the middle-line units.

The *support staff*, like the technostructure, lies outside the mainstream of the strategic apex, middle line, and operating core. This organizational component consists of specialized staff who provide support activities to the work of the organization. Support staff include legal advisors and housing, dining, administrative, computing, bookstore, printing, payroll, and student-affairs-units staff. Support staff do not teach or conduct basic research. They provide support services to those who engage in the teaching and research missions of the organization.

Using Mintzberg's framework of organizational structure, the institutional research office may be identified as part of the technostructure or support staff. Mintzberg reports that members of the technostructure are removed from the operating work flow. They may design, plan, change, and describe training needs of people to do the work, but they do not do it themselves. The work of those in the technostructure involves analytical studies that aid in standardizing and improving control over work processes, outputs, and personnel skills in the faculty operating core. Institutional researchers may be part of the technostructure if their primary role is to provide information and conduct research on such areas as long-range planning and environmental scanning. An institutional research office with a technostructure function and located in the strategic apex allows researchers to be closer to institutional boundaries with the external environment. This enhances opportunities for scanning the external environment for substantive changes in demographics, economic activity, social needs, and political interests. Information obtained by environmental scanning can alert members of the strategic apex to the need to change institutional strategies and policies.

The office of institutional research may instead be part of the support staff. Support staff units are found at all levels of the organization. Thus, institutional research as part of the support staff can be found at various levels of organizations. Support staff units provide specialized services to administrators, students, staff, and faculty. Institutional researchers are highly skilled and capable of providing specialized services in quantitative methods, computer programming, information technologies, data collection, and measurement techniques. The primary support service provided by institutional researchers is preparation and dissemination of information to external and internal interest groups. Conducting analytical studies and making reports to support the decisions of middle-line managers are fundamental duties of institutional researchers located in support-service units.

## Considerations for Locating an Institutional Research Office

Whether an institutional research office is a support service or a control agent in stabilizing and standardizing the work activities of an institution, size of the college or university is a fundamental consideration in deciding where to place such an office. As institutional size increases, the strategic apex becomes more concerned with external relations and financial problems and less concerned with coordination and direction of other administrators and academic work (Boland, 1971). Decision processes become less participatory and more likely to occur at the strategic apex with restricted opportunities for participation by students, middle-line units, and faculty. Thus, an increase in size brings a tendency to decentralize functions to more specialized units. There is more job specialization within units, more levels in the hierarchy, and a greater need for planning and control of work.

As institutions increase in size, the strategic apex knows less about the operating core. As planning and evaluation reports move up from the operating core to the middle line to the strategic apex, the reports are summarized, that is, increasingly less detailed. Consequently, the strategic apex lacks insights about academic processes and issues only brief communications regarding the organization's overall achievements and needs. In order to provide meaningful support to the work of the operating core in a large institution, middle-line managers have access to the communications network and work flow of both the strategic apex and the operating core. Therefore, institutional research offices that serve as a support-service unit located directly under the vice-president for academic affairs (a middle-line position) possess a view of the problems and information needs of all levels of the organization. Institutional researchers will improve their perception and understanding of the internal environment, but their knowledge of the external environment will be restricted. Here again, the institution should consider whether or not other suitable units could examine the institution's boundaries. If so, there is little need for an institutional research office to be assigned this technostructure responsibility.

The placement of an office of institutional research in a large university may not be congruent with the decision needs of a small college. For example, small colleges have less bureaucracy and fewer formal rules, specialized duties, and formal supervisory systems than large universities. Thus a desirable location for an institutional research office in a small college is under an executive administrator, such as the president or the executive vice-president of academic affairs. A centralized structure for small colleges, with the institutional research office located in the strategic apex, places this analytical and reporting office in an effective position in the work flow network, the communication network, and a friendship network. This key location allows an institutional research office to serve in the center of important communication networks between the president, vice-presidents, deans, department chairs, support units, faculty, and students.

Institutional research offices located under the vice-president for finance are expected to support the budgeting processes. Data needs for financial planning, resource allocation, and control become the pervading task for research offices under financial administration. The research office may be constrained from meeting adequately the information needs of other middle-line units responsible for academics, students, and general administration when thus located. However, the research office will gain influence by being placed under the power and influence of a financial vice-president.

An emerging location for the institutional research office is under an assistant vice-president in the offices of administration, finance, or academic affairs (Taylor, 1989). Locating the office below the vice-president level, however, raises serious questions about how important information gathering and reporting to meet the decision-making needs of the institution is considered to be. Placement of a research office at this level presents challenges to the staff to influence decision-making processes and to establish a central position in the communication network. Being in the center of the institution's communications network provides the institutional research office a significant opportunity to be aware of the information needs of a broad and influential group. Placing the research office under an assistant vice-president weakens the institution's ability to make considered judgments using valid and reliable information.

## Staffing an Institutional Research Office

Different types of staffing of institutional research offices have common features regardless of institution size and purpose. Because their purpose is to provide meaningful information in a timely manner for effective decision making, institutional research offices have developed a cadre of persons well trained in analytical methods and information-retrieval skills. These skills are most often obtained through formal programs in business, educational research, mathematics, and the social sciences. The Association for Institutional Research has become a key resource for meeting the professional needs of institutional researchers by providing workshops and annual association programs to introduce and advance the knowledge and practice of institutional research.

There has been a move away from selecting institutional research staff who have keen insights into the academic processes that occur in the faculty operating core. While many institutional research directors hold a doctorate as their highest degree, primarily in the social sciences and education, very few have assigned teaching duties (Taylor, 1989; Volkwein, Agrotes, and Hannahs, 1989). As an institution increases in size, the need for a continuous flow of information to the strategic apex and middle-line units becomes intense. Institutional research directors have responded to these demands for information and planning by staffing their offices with persons well trained in quantitative methods (Taylor, 1989). Consequently, the responsibility to analyze problems associated with teaching and research has been given to the school and department level in the form of faculty committees and consultants. Thus, institutional research staff are not now always in the best position to respond to the new challenge provided by recent increased interest in assessing student learning. Chapter Seven in this volume provides some guidelines for offices charged with initiating an assessment process for the first time.

Movement of an institutional research office to another location within the organization's structure may create a need for changes in staff. While institutional researchers need generic knowledge and skills in quantitative and information retrieval methods, the contextual knowledge and skills needed may change if the institutional research office is subject to relocation with each turnover of the top administration. Such changes with each administration can result in incongruencies in work expectations and job specialization skills of those currently employed in the institutional research office. Currently, as major issues shift at individual institutions (such as recruitment and retention of students, equal-education opportunities, student outcomes assessment, or accreditation-report needs), involvement and work expectations of the institutional researchers also shift.

## Some Final Observations

Successful offices of institutional research are designed and located to fit a logical organizational configuration and associated situational factors. Institutional research offices have suffered over the years as a result of being located on the basis of personalities and special-interest groups. As institutions have increased in size, age, and traditions, the institutional research office has moved lower in the organizational hierarchy. Compounding the uncertainty of where to locate an institutional research office within the organizational structure to make it successful and effective is the problem of frequent turnover of executive administrators. Stability of location for an institutional research office becomes more assured as the office is placed lower in the organizational hierarchy where there tends to be less administrative turnover.

In small colleges, an institutional research office can function effectively at the strategic apex as part of the president's office. While the faculty operating core may be suspicious of any unit attached to the strategic apex, this location provides the opportunity for the institutional research office to develop friendship networks with administrators and faculty to moderate any distrust that might arise.

As institutions increase in size, the institutional research office can be more effective if located in a position to develop comprehensive networks in the midst of the institution's communication network. The middle-line unit of vice-president is a location where information exchanges occur between the strategic apex, middle line, and faculty operating core. Support information from service units with many specialized functions flows through the middle line to the higher levels of administration. Since the fundamental work of a college or university is academic, a desirable location for an institutional research office in large institutions is under the vice-president for academic affairs. Information about budgets, students, faculty, facilities, curriculum, libraries, and other features of academia come together under the vice-president for academic affairs. Locating the institutional research office under a vice-president for academic affairs allows the institutional research staff to become knowledgeable, comprehensive, and perceptive about the academic and support processes involved in educating students as well as about faculty research. In this location, the staff are in a position to develop friendship networks with faculty and student leadership organizations as well as with administrators at different hierarchical levels. The specialized staff required to work under these conditions include those with skills in quantitative methods and information technology as well as an understanding of academic processes, the nature of faculty work, and student learning, a comprehensive understanding of the curriculum, and awareness of political conflicts within the institution.

Institutional researchers need to have access to information regarding the decision-making needs of their institution and therefore need to be in a position where this access is most convenient for them, if they are to do their best work.

## References

Boland, W. R. "Size, Organization, and Environmental Mediation: A Study of Colleges and Universities." In J. V. Baldridge (ed.), *Academic Governance.* Berkeley, Calif.: McCutchan, 1971.

Brass, D. J. "Being in the Right Place: A Structural Analysis of Individual Influence in an Organization." *Administrative Science Quarterly,* 1984, 29 (4), 518–539.

James, L. R., and Jones, A. P. "Organizational Structure: A Review of Structural Dimensions and Their Relationships with Individual Attitudes and Behavior." *Organizational Behavior and Human Performance,* 1976, *16,* 74–113.

Mintzberg, H. *Structure in Fives: Designing Effective Organizations.* Englewood Cliffs, N.J.: Prentice-Hall, 1983.

Saupe, J. L. *The Functions of Institutional Research.* (2nd ed.) Tallahassee, Fla.: Association for Institutional Research, 1990.

Taylor, A. L. "Organizational Structure and Institutional Research Role and Function." Paper presented at the 29th Annual Forum of the Association for Institutional Research, Baltimore, Md., April 30–May 3, 1989.

Volkwein, J. F., Agrotes, M., and Hannahs, D. "The Structure and Functions of Institutional Research Offices Within NEAIR." *North East Association for Institutional Research 16th Annual Conference Proceedings,* Pittsburgh, Pa., October 21–24, 1989.

*Alton L. Taylor is a professor in the Center for the Study of Higher Education and director of the summer session at the University of Virginia.*

*An open-systems framework gives focus to the nature and scope of institutional research.*

# The Nature and Scope of Institutional Research

*Michael F. Middaugh*

No one I know has ever said to me that he or she aspired from childhood to a career in institutional research. Yet thousands of us practice the trade across the country, and hundreds of newcomers join the field each year. Over the past thirty years, the emergence of institutional research as a central tool in data-based decision and policy making at colleges and universities argues strongly that it has matured as a component of management practice (Saupe, 1990). Relevant models can be developed to describe the practice of institutional research in most types of postsecondary institutions. The purpose of this chapter is to develop one such descriptive model. Specifically, this chapter proposes a working definition for institutional research, describes a conceptual framework for applying institutional research to the study of colleges and universities and key issues for institutional research, and discusses resources to aid in the analysis of data variables.

## Definition of Institutional Research

What exactly is institutional research, and why do we do it? To answer that question, we must understand the information needs of colleges and universities, particularly with respect to policy and decision making. Jones (1982) describes the role of data and information in shaping policy within a turbulent organizational environment. His discussion helps understand the role of institutional research in that process. Institutional research must play a focal role in addressing three questions central to the continued survival of any organization:

• *Where is the organization at this moment?* Specifically, what is the "fit" between a college or university's mission and its current programs and services? What is the institution's position within the educational marketplace? Who are the competition, and what are they doing?

• *Where is the organization going?* What potential changes in the environment may affect the institution? What changes in the programs and services would make them more consistent with the institution's mission and more reflective of changing environmental conditions?

• *How can the organization best arrive at its desired end?* What alternative courses of action are available to the institution in pursuing its objectives? What costs are associated with implementing the various alternatives? Can the institution afford to act? Can the institution afford not to act?

These three general questions serve as a foundation for the following working definition of institutional research:

> Institutional research is the sum total of all activities directed at empirically describing the full spectrum of functions (educational, administrative, and support) at a college or university. Institutional research activities examine those functions in their broadest definitions and, in the context of both internal and external environments, embrace data collection and analytical strategies in support of decision making at the institution.

To be of value in the decision support and planning, institutional research cannot be a patchwork quilt of ad hoc research projects reacting to specific questions asked by senior campus administrators (Suslow, 1973; Saupe, 1990). Institutional research must have a structured view of organizational activity and a process for analyzing that view that has an integrity of its own (Petersen, 1985). To achieve that structured view, a conceptual framework for thinking about organizations and how they function is important.

## Conceptual Framework and Key Issues for Institutional Research

An extremely useful way of looking at colleges and universities (or any organization, for that matter) is to think of them as "open systems." Essentially, this theory proposes that all organizations are comprised of three central components: inputs, processes, and outputs. In order to function and remain viable, any organization must continuously secure personnel, raw materials, fiscal and physical resources, and other types of inputs, which the organization then acts on (processes) to create a product (output). An ongoing series of transactions with the external environment is central to the theory (Aldrich, 1979; Hall, 1987). The environment supplies the raw materials (inputs) and serves as the ultimate determinant of organizational success through consumption of organizational products. Figure 1 illustrates the open-systems concept within the context of higher education.

Some argue that an open-systems view of organizational activity, long the norm in industry, employs terminology ("inputs," "processes," "outputs") that is inappropriate for higher education. Semantics aside, closer examination suggests that the open-systems model is not only relevant to education but may be essential if colleges and universities are to be effective within the larger environmental context. The following discussion illustrates the point.

**Inputs.** Consider the inputs into the higher educational enterprise. What are the basic "raw materials" a college or university needs in order to function? Clearly, students, faculty, and staff are essential. Buildings are needed for teaching, research, and conducting other educational business. Fiscal and physical resources are needed to pay salaries, equip classrooms and laboratories, and fund other business-related activities. Institutional research describes these inputs in a way that answers such fundamental questions as: Who or what are they? How many are there? and What do they look like? For example, the following basic information is essential for an accurate description of the inputs into the higher education system:

• *Students:* How many matriculated and nonmatriculated students are enrolled? How many are full-time students and how many are part-time? Undergraduate and graduate? First-time and transfer? What are their general demographic and academic profiles?

• *Faculty:* How many full-time and part-time faculty are employed at the institution? What is the highest degree held by each faculty member

**Figure 1. Conceptual Framework for Analysis of University Functions**

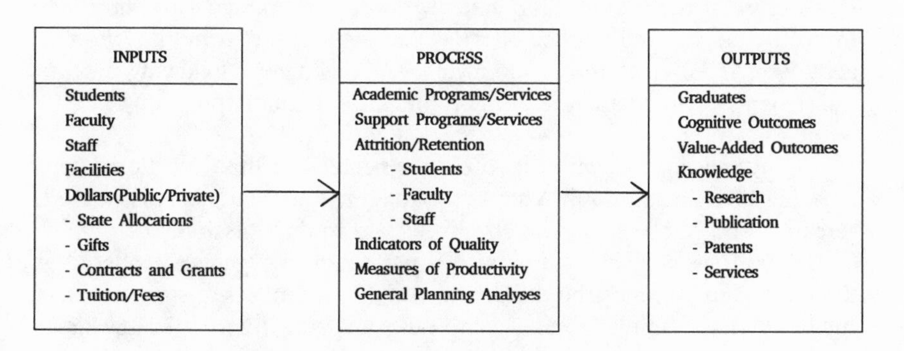


EXTERNAL ENVIRONMENT

-Fiscal/Economic considerations
-Marketplace considerations
-Governmental/Regulatory considerations
-Other considerations

and from what institution? What is the age profile of the faculty? Does the faculty represent the desired ethnic and cultural diversity? Is the institution successfully attracting the best and brightest scholars available?

• *Staff:* The same broad questions about faculty are also appropriate for staff. Is the institution attracting the best possible personnel to support the educational process?

• *Facilities:* How many buildings on how many acres comprise the campus? What is the age and general condition of the buildings? What is the gross versus the net square footage in each building? How efficiently are classrooms and other instructional spaces utilized? What is the need for bringing new facilities on line or for refurbishing existing facilities?

• *Financial resources:* What proportion of institutional revenues come from tuition and fees? From government appropriations? From contracts and grants? From gifts? From other sources? How "tuition dependent" is the institution? How has the funding pattern changed over time? What is the relative strength of each of the revenue streams into the institution?

It is difficult to imagine a college or university surviving for very long without a basic knowledge and understanding of the issues described above (Jonsen, 1984; Chaffee, 1984). Institutional research, through sound data management and systematic analysis, provides such basic information on inputs reliably and consistently.

**Process.** Questions about process are similar to those about inputs. Federal and state agencies, often under the aegis of assessment mandates, are asking colleges and universities to provide evidence that students have grown intellectually during their college years (Ewell, 1985; Jacobi, Astin, and Ayala, 1987). Boards of trustees, financial auditors, and occasionally consumer groups call upon higher education institutions to demonstrate efficiency, effectiveness, and economy in their operations. Process questions, which are far more difficult to answer than those regarding inputs, include: What is the institution actually doing with inputs? How are those inputs being changed by the college experience? Is the institution doing a good job? An efficient and economical job? Consider the following process issues, which can be analyzed only through a systematic program of institutional research:

• *Institutional mission:* What are the objectives of the educational process at a given institution? What is the intended emphasis on instruction, research, and public service, respectively, within that mission?

• *Academic programs and services:* What degree programs are offered at the institution? What is the depth and breadth of services to support those programs (for example: library, computing, advising, tutoring)? How satisfied are the consumers of these programs and services? Can intellectual and experiential gains, attributable to the college experience, be estimated or measured?

• *Other programs and services:* What services are offered to meet the full range of needs of *both* students and employees (for example: extracurricular activities, career planning and placement, personal counseling, health and wellness services, midcareer renewal opportunities)? How satisfied are the consumers of these services?

• *Completion:* To what extent do inputs (students, faculty, and staff) complete the process for which they were recruited? That is, how many students graduate and how many employees remain until retirement? For what reasons do some inputs fail to reach completion?

• *Productivity:* Do sensible strategies exist for measuring academic administrative productivity? What common units of measurement have been defined? Is it possible to distinguish accurately between a "lean" and a "rich" operation?

• *Quality:* Can quality, as it applies to any aspect of the academic enterprise, be measured? If so, how? Is it possible to obtain comparative measures of quality from other institutions?

• *Strategic and budget planning:* How can process data be most effectively used in defining institutional direction and in allocating resources to achieve that direction?

As the competition for scarce resources for higher education becomes more intense, the most successful colleges and universities will be those that clearly demonstrate their value to the larger society. That value will be measured, largely through institutional research activity, in terms of the quality of the educational process and the products it generates.

**Outputs.** What are the tangible products of the higher education process? Does the process merit ongoing investment? Institutional research plays a central role in answering these questions through a full description of the outputs, or end products of the higher education process. The following issues are worthy of consideration:

• *Graduates:* How many students graduate from the institution each year, with which degrees, and in which disciplines? What is the initial rate of post-graduation employment or graduate-school placement? To what extent do graduates of the institution feel that their college experience has relevance to their post-graduation activity?

• *Cognitive outcomes:* What demonstrable cognitive gains can be measured in those who are processed through the college or university experience?

• *"Value-added" outcomes:* What behavioral or attitudinal changes can be attributed directly or indirectly to the college or university experience?

• *Other outcomes:* To what extent is the institution contributing to the body of knowledge, as measured in terms of such activities as research, contracts and grants, publications, patents, and public service?

**Environmental Considerations.** Simply measuring inputs, process, and outputs is a major task in and of itself. However, the most significant aspect of the open-systems framework is acknowledging that the environment has a profound impact on the institution's ability to perform its system functions. Environmental issues raise another series of questions:

• *Marketplace considerations:* What is the institution's position in the admissions, recruiting, and faculty recruiting marketplaces? What are other institutions doing to affect that position? Are enrollment and staffing strategies and projections consistent with marketplace considerations? How is the marketplace likely to change during the next five years? During the next ten to twenty years?

• *Fiscal and economic considerations:* What is the institution's overall fiscal condition? What have been the trends with respect to revenue and expenditure streams for critical institutional functions (for example: instruction, academic support, student support, financial aid, facilities maintenance). How well has the institution invested its resources? How do institutional income and expenditure patterns compare with those of peer institutions? How will external factors such as inflation and interest rates likely affect the institution?

• *Government and regulatory considerations:* How do government regulations, ranging from affirmative action to asbestos abatement affect the organization? How do mandates from external agencies (such as outcomes assessment, NCAA [National Collegiate Athletic Association] compliance, federal and state reporting requirements) affect operations?

• *Other:* In what other ways do aspects of the environment (for example "town-and-gown" considerations) have an impact on the college or university's operations?

Just as natural selection promotes the survival of those species with characteristics that are adaptable to the environment, so too will adaptable institutions survive (Aldrich, 1979; Cameron, 1984). Adaptability, in the instance of organizations, is not a random event. It is a function of an institution's capacity to understand the integrity of its own mission, the organizational processes that drive toward the realization of that mission, and the extent to which the external environment imposes opportunities and constraints on those processes. Institutional research can be thought of as the central key to that understanding.

## Resources for Analysis

Having examined the central components of the open-systems model, it is then possible to establish a set of concrete measures to quantify inputs, processes, outputs, and organizational transactions with the external environment. Table 1 presents some base-line measures for each system component. The listing in Table 1 is not exhaustive; it is a starting point. Individual offices of institutional research will add and delete items as their individual circumstances dictate. Similarly, the research effort at any given point in time will likely embrace only portions of the listing, again as institutional circumstances mandate.

**Table 1. Selected Institutional Research Measures of Organizational Inputs, Processes, and Outputs Within a Higher Education Context**

| *Systemic Component* | *Selected Measures* | |
|---|---|---|
| *Inputs* | | |
| Students | Headcount | Ethnicity |
| | Full-/part-time status | Geographic origin |
| | Full-time equivalency | High school GPA |
| | Sex | SAT/ACT scores |
| | Age | Other |
| Faculty and staff | Headcount | Ethnicity |
| | Full-/part-time status | Highest degree |
| | Full-time equivalency | Entry salary |
| | Sex | Tenure status |
| | Age | Other |
| Facilities | Campus acreage | Space inventory |
| | Buildings owned/leased | Utilization rates |
| | Gross square footage | Deferred maintenance |
| | Net square footage | Other |
| Revenues | Tuition and fees | Gifts |
| | Government appropriations | Other |
| | Contracts and grants | |
| *Processes* | | |
| Institutional mission, academic and support programs | Degree program inventory | |
| | Course inventory | |
| | Support program inventory | |
| | Program utilization studies | |
| | Student satisfaction studies | |
| | Accreditation studies | |
| | Faculty/staff "quality-of-life" studies | |
| | Institutional and professional program | |
| | Other | |
| Completion | Retention/attrition analyses | |
| | Graduation analyses | |
| | Faculty retention analyses | |
| | Exiting faculty/staff studies | |
| | Withdrawing/nonreturning student analyses | |
| | Other | |
| Productivity | Grade distribution analyses | |
| | Instructional workload analyses | |
| | Student credit hours | |
| | Full time equivalent (FTE) | |
| | Students and faculty | |
| | Student-faculty ratio | |
| | Teaching contact hours | |
| | Other | |

**Table 1.** *(continued)*

| *Systemic Component* | *Selected Measures* |
|---|---|
| Productivity (*continued*) | Faculty effort reports<br>Research grant/patent activity studies<br>Other |
| Quality | Institutional and professional program<br>Accreditations<br>Reputational ranking of academic programs<br>Other |
| Strategic/budget planning | Trends in revenues and expenditures<br>Financial ratio analysis of institutional financial statement and balance sheet<br>Other |
| *Outputs* | |
| Graduates | Degrees-granted studies<br>Post-graduation activity analysis<br>Alumni follow-up studies<br>Other |
| Cognitive outcomes | Grade distribution studies<br>Cognitive gain testing<br>Other |
| Value-added outcomes | College student experience analyses<br>Other |
| Institutional outputs | Research grant/patent inventory<br>Faculty publications directory<br>Faculty public service inventory<br>Other |
| *Environmental Considerations* | |
| Marketplace factors | Admissions marketing analyses<br>Faculty/staff availability analyses<br>Comparative compensation studies<br>High school enrollment projections<br>Admissions yield projections<br>U.S. census demographic projections<br>Other |

**Table 1.** *(continued)*

| *Systemic Component* | *Selected Measures* |
|---|---|
| *Environmental Considerations (continued)* | |
| *Fiscal factors* | Consumer price index projections<br>Educational price index projections<br>Regional economic analyses (including economic impact studies)<br>Other |

Once appropriate measures of inputs, outputs, processes, and organizational environment have been established, strategies for data collection must be developed. For example, analyses of admissions and personnel-recruiting activity, student persistence, staffing patterns, instructional workload, student and employee satisfaction, and general educational outcomes are all essential tasks in developing a program of institutional research from this framework. At first glance, the prospect of assembling and analyzing data to complete these studies might seem overwhelming. Most new practitioners of institutional research, in particular, are relatively unaware of the broad array of data collection resources available to them. These resources include prepared data sets, commercially developed data collection instruments, data-sharing consortia of higher education institutions, and professional associations and publications. A brief review of these resources will animate the framework for institutional research discussed thus far.

Defining the discrete pieces of data associated with the measures listed in Table 1 must include the full range of activity within the higher education institution. Equally important is ensuring a commonality in the data definitions that will permit inter-institutional comparisons. The National Center for Higher Education Management Systems (NCHEMS) has developed a publication that casts crucial data elements in common definitions (Christal and Jones, 1982).

The starting point for data collection is with the institution's own data bases. The student record system, course registration file, personnel data base, budget file, or facilities file may contain many, if not most, of the data elements needed for developing the measures outlined in Table 1. Data element dictionaries, available from the campus computing center, will describe data base structures and accessing procedures. For those institutions that do not have reliable data bases, it is possible for institutional research offices to build their own. Many computer software vendors have data base templates for desktop personal computers. NCHEMS and Vantage Information Products developed a series of templates under their *Decision Support Series* addressing admissions, faculty, financial planning, and other areas. Other vendors offering similar packages advertise regularly in trade journals. Institutional research offices need only populate these frameworks with local data. Jennifer Wilton in Chapter Four provides further information and guidelines for organizing access to institutional data bases, and Karen L. Miselis addresses the management of data in Chapter Five.

Standard governmental reporting documents are another rich source of data. The Integrated Postsecondary Educational Data System (IPEDS), formerly known as the Higher Education General Information System (HEGIS), is operated by the U.S. Department of Education. Virtually all colleges and universities in the nation report data to IPEDS, and the system was expanded in 1987 to include proprietary institutions. IPEDS reports include fall semester enrollment data (by level, sex, and ethnicity), degrees granted (by discipline and ethnicity), financial activity (current funds, revenues, expenditures, and transfers), and personnel (by job classification, sex, and ethnicity). If institutional data bases are used to develop these reports, they can be further massaged to yield additional subgroupings and breakouts. If the reports are prepared by hand, as is sometimes the case in smaller institutions, the data may be entered into electronic spreadsheets for future use in developing trend lines.

IPEDS data lend themselves to inter-institutional comparisons. John Minter Associates of Boulder, Colorado, has taken HEGIS and IPEDS data over time for most colleges and universities in the country, grouped them by institutional type using the Carnegie classification, and developed comparative data available in both hard copy and diskette format. Data are available for admissions, enrollments, general institutional characteristics, fund raising, and finances, among others. Minter utilizes the concept of ratio analysis in developing data sets, a technique that is particularly useful in assessing institutional finances (Minter and others, 1987).

Massaging data bases is quickly and easily accomplished using statistical software packages and electronic spreadsheets. While a myriad of software packages, tailored to specific situations and circumstances, are commercially available from a variety of vendors, a few emerge as the standards. Among statistical software packages, SPSS (Statistical Package for the Social Sciences) and SAS (Statistical Analysis System) are most widely used. Each is user friendly, easy to learn, remarkably powerful in its range of statistics, and available in both mainframe and personal computer versions. Among electronic spreadsheets, Lotus Corporation offers basic spreadsheet, graphics, and statistical capabilities. Other vendors offer packages designed to link with LOTUS to provide enhanced spreadsheet capabilities. The NCHEMS Decision Support Series, described earlier, is designed to run in concert with LOTUS. It is not uncommon to find sophisticated student flow models, revenue projection models, and budget forecasting models operating in a spreadsheet environment in offices of institutional research.

The discussion thus far has focused on identification, collection, and massaging of commercially prepared data or data that already exist in the institution. Occasionally, essential data are not available in the institution's data bases and must be collected via survey, interview, or other external data collection techniques. Student satisfaction surveys, attitudinal questionnaires, and alumni surveys collect such data. Most experienced institutional researchers try to avoid developing in-house surveys and questionnaires because of the burden of establishing estimates of validity and reliability. It is more efficient to employ instruments that commercial vendors have developed that address a broad spectrum of data collection needs and have satisfied the validity and reliability issues. The Educational Testing Service and the American College Testing Program are representative of companies that provide instruments to assess cognitive gains, student satisfaction with programs and services, reasons students leave without graduating, alumni perceptions of the relevance of the college experience, and other institutional questions and concerns. Each has a catalog and specimen set available from the address at the end of this chapter. The University of California, Los Angeles, offers two other highly useful surveys. Alexander Astin's Cooperative Institutional Research Project uses a standardized student information form to collect demographic and attitudinal data from first-time freshmen. Astin's group then develops national norms for various institutional types against which specific college and university scores can be compared. Robert Pace developed the College Student Experiences Questionnaire, which is an excellent vehicle for assessing students' self-estimated gains as a result of the college experience. Again, contact addresses are listed at the end of the chapter.

Perhaps the greatest resource available to institutional researchers is other colleagues in the field. When a specific data collection or analysis problem defies all conventional wisdom to be found in books and journals, the capacity to tap into a collegial network of individuals who have faced and solved similar problems is invaluable. The Association for Institutional Research (AIR) is the national professional association for institutional researchers. Its Annual Forum brings together colleagues from across the nation and the world to hear featured speakers, contributed papers, symposia, and workshops on virtually every aspect of the institutional research profession. AIR has a number of affiliated regional associations that tend to be informal, closely knit, and easily accessible. Information on AIR and the regional associations can be obtained from the AIR national office. The Society for College and University Planning (SCUP) is another national organization whose programs are becoming increasingly attractive to institutional researchers. Both addresses are found at the end of the chapter.

## Summary

The purpose of this chapter has been to provide a general framework for viewing the nature and scope of institutional research. Using an open-systems approach to studying organizational functions, we have cast the open-systems model in a higher education context to describe the central issues for institutional research. Having developed the framework, we then provided resources for collecting and analyzing data and discussed resources to which the institutional researcher can turn for additional assistance.

## Additional Resources

American College Testing Program
P.O. Box 168
Iowa City, Iowa 52243

Alexander Astin
c/o Cooperative Institutional Research Project
University of California
Los Angeles, California 90024

Educational Testing Service
Princeton, New Jersey 08541

Lotus Corporation
55 Cambridge Parkway
Cambridge, Massachusetts 02142

John Minter Associates
2400 Central Avenue, Suite B-2
Boulder, Colorado 80301

National Center for Higher Education
Management Systems
P.O. Box Drawer P
Boulder, Colorado 80302

C. Robert Pace
c/o Center for Study of Evaluation
University of California
Los Angeles, California 90024

SAS, Inc.
Box 8000
Cary, North Carolina 27511

SPSS, Inc.
444 North Michigan Avenue, Suite 3000
Chicago, Illinois 60611

***Organizations***

Association for Institutional Research
314 Stone Building
Florida State University
Tallahassee, Florida 32306

Society for College and University Planning
2026M School of Education Building
University of Michigan
Ann Arbor, Michigan 48106

## References


Aldrich, H. E. *Organizations and Environments.* Englewood Cliffs, N.J: Prentice-Hall, 1979.

Cameron, K. S. "Organizational Adaptation and Higher Education." *Journal of Higher Education,* 1984, *55* (2), 122–144.

Chaffee, E. E. "Successful Strategic Management in Small Private Colleges." *Journal of Higher Education,* 1984, *55* (2), 212–241.

Christal, E., and Jones, P. *A Common Language for Post-Secondary Accreditation: Categories and Definitions for Data Collection.* Boulder, Colo.: National Center for Higher Education Management Systems, 1982.

Ewell, P. T. (ed.). *Assessing Educational Outcomes.* New Directions for Institutional Research, no. 47. San Francisco: Jossey-Bass, 1985.

Hall, R. H. *Organizations: Structures, Processes, and Outcomes.* Englewood Cliffs, N.J.: Prentice-Hall, 1987.

Jacobi, M., Astin, A., and Ayala, F. *College Student Outcomes Assessment: A Talent Development Perspective.* ASHE-ERIC Higher Education Report, no. 7. Washington, D.C.: ERIC Clearinghouse on Higher Education and the Association for the Study of Higher Education, 1987.

Jones, D. P. *Data and Information for Executive Decisions in Higher Education.* Boulder, Colo.: National Center for Higher Education Management Systems, 1982.

Jonsen, R. W. "Small Colleges Cope with the Eighties: Sharp Eye on the Horizon, Strong Hand on the Tiller." *Journal of Higher Education,* 1984, *55* (2), 171–183.

Minter, J., Hughes, K. S., Robinson, D. D., Turk, F. J., Parager, F. J., and Buchanan, A. D. *Ratio Analysis in Higher Education.* New York: Peat, Marwick, and Main, 1987.

Peterson, M. W. "Institutional Research: An Evolutionary Perspective." In M. W. Peterson and M. Corcoran (eds.), *Institutional Research in Transition.* New Directions for Institutional Research, no. 46. San Francisco: Jossey-Bass, 1985.

Saupe, J. L. *The Functions of Institutional Research.* (2nd ed.) Tallahassee, Fla.: Association for Institutional Research, 1990.

Suslow, S. *A Declaration on Institutional Research.* Tallahassee Fla.: ESSO Education Foundation and Association for Institutional Research, 1972.

*Michael F. Middaugh is director of institutional research and planning at the University of Delaware and served as president of the North East Association for Institutional Research in 1989–1990.*

*Reporting is not only important, it's rather like housework—as soon as you think you have finished, it's time to start all over again.*

# Organizing for Reporting

*Jennifer Wilton*

Reporting occupies a central place among the responsibilities of most institutional research offices. Indeed, Volkwein reports in Chapter One that more than 80 percent of institutional research offices are involved in reporting enrollment data and student characteristics, supplying national survey data, answering college guidebook surveys, and responding to state-related requests for data. Reporting is not a glamorous task and receives far fewer accolades than deserved, since it consumes more resources than appears warranted on the surface. On the other hand, a sound reporting capacity provides the basis for research and planning, and reporting, although often a tedious job, is the very essence of knowing the institution. It is the aim of this chapter to offer some suggestions and guidelines on how to set up a reporting capability and keep at a minimum the amount of time and other resources that must be spent on this important activity.

## Reporting in the Context of Institutional Research

In order for managers and administrators to be able to meet productively and reach agreement on issues of policy and planning with respect to their institution, they must keep to a minimum the time spent settling the issue of which information is valid as a basis for decisions. The implication of this is that progress will be much greater where there is a source of information that is accepted as correct both officially and in practice (Borden and Delaney, 1989). This situation may be achieved in different ways depending on the structure and policies of the institution. In an institution that is comprised of a loose federation of colleges that set many of their own policies, authority for reporting official statistics may rest in individual colleges, while in an institution that is more centrally organized, a single office may be the recognized source. Whatever the structure, for effective use of information in decision making

- There should be one set of statistics that is recognized as official
- The mission of the office(s) charged with producing and reporting these statistics should be clear and supported by the administration
- The data must be demonstrably correct
- Wherever appropriate, these should be the data used by members of the institution for decision making.

In order for this to occur with a minimum of conflict, the charge of the producing office must be clear to all concerned, and that office must be competent to perform its task.

For purposes of this chapter, reporting is defined as the assembly of information from institutional data bases rather than from surveys, samples, or approximations. It demands as close to complete accuracy as possible and must allow reliable comparison over time. This type of reporting entails having access to the operational data of an institution. Exactly how that access is set up and how it is used influences not only how time is spent but also the training and expertise needed by the institutional research office staff.

Reporting data may pertain to students, employees, budgetary information, or facilities, and reports may range from such simple information as the number of applications received in a given time period to complex tracking of faculty workload. The forms reporting takes may be dictated from outside the institution, may sometimes even consist of raw-data files created to fixed specifications on computer media, or may consist of fairly informal ad hoc statistics, generated to meet an immediate institutional need.

Before the advent of computerized data bases, reporting effort was a function of size, with larger institutions needing more staff for manual compilation of statistics. With the growth in administrative computing, however, the largest institutions often have the most sophisticated systems and central support and are in the best position to respond to new external and internal requests for information. In a computerized environment it takes virtually the same effort to organize a data set to report on 500 students as it does on 15,000. Currently, it is in smaller institutions where the task is likely to be most difficult. The institutional researcher working alone undertakes all aspects of reporting as well as other tasks. In addition, other resources such as hardware, software, and expertise are likely to be harder to obtain (Glover, 1988). State funding that helps defray the cost of new types of mandated reports should not be allocated in direct proportion to institutional size.

**Standardizing Reporting.** For reporting to be useful either to the institution or to outside agencies, reports must be comparable across time. If enrollments have declined between one fall and the next, the reports must ensure that this change is not a function of either changing definitions or the point in time when the data were assembled.

In order to achieve comparability of data between reference points, a census of data at a consistent point in time must be taken. This usually needs the cooperation of the institutional researcher, data-processing personnel, and operational offices to make a copy, or "snapshot," of the relevant institutional data. These snapshots can then be used as a series of points in time, and form the basis not only for accurate semesterly or yearly reporting, but also research studies.

Census data can represent a relative point in time or a standard period of time. The IPEDS (Integrated Postsecondary Education Data Systems) Enrollment Report, on the one hand, asks for enrollments "as of the institution's official fall reporting date," which represents a *relative point in time*. Completions, on the other hand, are defined, for most purposes, as those awards conferred between July 1 of one year and June 30 of the next; in other words, for a *standard period of time*. There are various methods for achieving these standards. Information may be extracted directly from a computerized system using a standard marker such as a flag or date; data files may be created by production programs run by a central data processing group at agreed-upon times; reports may even be compiled from paper lists provided by offices. Deciding on the best method will be based on factors peculiar to the individual institution, although some guidelines are offered later in this chapter.

Standard measures are as important to reporting as standard timing but unfortunately much harder to achieve. There are three tasks: first, to make sure that definitions are consistent across time and between reports; second, to work closely with other offices to minimize the impact of any changes that may be made in how data are collected, entered, or stored; and third, to be part of a communication network that transmits policy developments that might influence the interpretation of changes in numbers over time. Even if the office has little influence over such changes, staff need to be aware of them since they will profoundly affect the interpretation of the data. Reporting is more than merely generating correct information; it is also being aware of the meaning and implication of that information.

**Substantive Areas of Reporting.** A major domain for reporting concerns student data on admissions, including recruitment; student performance, particularly where an institution is involved in assessment; enrollment; and completions. Due to the demands of the admissions and registration process at most institutions and the availability of customized software, these data are likely to be in computerized form, and access and tools for data retrieval present fewer problems than with most other data. On the other hand, the institutional researcher may spend a great deal of time unravelling complications that can wreak havoc with reporting but that are happily accepted by operational offices because they do not affect day to day efficiency. For many institutional researchers, reporting student data will consume the majority of reporting resources.

A second domain concerns organizational information, which falls into the categories of employee, course, and program information. For many institutions the tasks of generating information on employees and on students will be similar since a campus that has automated any of its data systems is likely to have done so for both of these. While issues of security and access may arise when dealing with personnel data, course and program data are more likely to be located on paper records than electronic media. In addition they are often less precise, since these data, particularly in historical form, are not of daily importance to management. Deans who care passionately about how many new freshmen are enrolled in English 101 are quite lukewarm about whether it is the same course as the old English 010. The institutional researcher may be in the lonely position of being the only person who cares about the date on which the institution first offered a bachelor's degree in engineering, although quite a few people will be interested in how many students the institution has graduated with that degree since then.

While official financial reporting is not within the purview of institutional research, some are involved in resource analysis (44 percent in the Volkwein study reported in Chapter One). Financial information is likely to be the most carefully maintained, but at the same time it is extremely sensitive and hence requires most security procedures for access.

Other information that was thought would not be needed may become important at any time. Reporting on facilities use may seem unnecessary, but as soon as the data are excluded from the information plan, someone will want to prove that a new building is either needed or not needed. Campus security logs, student housing information, and other apparently obscure data sources can become crucial in meeting a sudden management information need. To an office that has a good grasp of the basic data and available tools (both hardware and software), such occurrences become an opportunity to broaden the reporting base rather than a burden.

The bonus at the end of organizing to create a good reporting function in these areas is an institutional research office with a thorough grasp of the institution's data and an information system that contains the raw material for future research. If the reporting data are organized into a coherent data system such as a series of SPSS-X or SAS files, or even, where expertise permits, a relational database system, the institution has the core data base for many research projects.

## Organizing to Create the Reporting Data Base

Aspects that need to be considered when creating a reporting data base are discussed in this section. These aspects include locating appropriate data, documentation of available data sources, getting data into usable form, and working with data processing personnel.

**Locating Appropriate Data.** The place to start an investigation is with the purpose of the report. For example, if a college of engineering keeps its own records of students completing requirements for a master's degree in engineering in addition to the official data base kept by the registrar, which should be used? The answer depends largely on whether you need to know how many students completed the requirements for an engineering degree or how many master's degrees in engineering the institution awarded. These are both legitimate, but quite different, questions. When deciding on a possible source of data, asking the following questions can avoid wasted time:

- Do you need "official" institutional data to answer this question? If so, pursue them. If not, explore other sources.
- Are the data in a form that enables you to create the report rapidly and accurately? Rekeying data should be avoided whenever possible.
- Are the data accessible by your office, or can they be made so? If data exist that are preferable but not presently accessible, you may opt to use those that are available while working to obtain access to the preferred source.
- Are the data valid and reliable? Again one may consider working with inferior data while striving to improve or change the source. Learning when to spend time insisting on total accuracy and when to accept a certain amount of unavoidable error is extremely important. Some strategies for evaluating data quality will be offered later in this chapter.

**Documentation.** One of the most important tools when organizing a new reporting data base is documentation of the available data sources. The problem is how to know whether the documentation is accurate. This is an extremely pertinent question, but unfortunately one without a palatable answer. In almost all cases some kind of documentation will be available, either through an official data dictionary, if the institution has a computerized data base, or through training and reference material used by those offices responsible for maintaining the data.

- If you cannot understand what you have, you should find someone to explain it. Documentation often leaves out what "everyone knows," and it is only when a new person asks questions that this comes to light.
- If the documentation does not tell you everything you need to know, you should ask questions. There are usually addenda, errata, extra coding sheets, and other "nonessential" information for any system that has been in operation for a while.

• Ultimately, the only way to test the documentation is to use it. If your dictionary lists six codes for race and the data yield eight, you should be suspicious of the six that appear to be correct. If you are in the fortunate (and unlikely) position that everything you examine fits the codes, you can relax a little. Unfortunately this type of testing takes a great deal of time and effort.

Confidence in the documentation is achieved only over a period of time. Improving documentation and data quality should be high on your agenda.

**Getting the Data into Usable Form.** One method of collecting data, a relic from before the days of extensive computerization, is to request information from other departments by providing them with forms to complete or asking them for paper output. The office then compiles its final reports from this input, either by hand or with the assistance of spreadsheet software. In small, noncomputerized institutions this practice may be inevitable, but wherever possible it should be phased out. Inherent problems include the following:

- The institutional research office cannot exercise data quality control. Items cannot even be cross-checked.
- Definitions are also in others' hands and may not be consistent with each other and across time.
- The method is time-consuming and prone to error.
- The process may create an adversarial relationship. At the busiest time of the year, a memo arrives asking for a form to be completed. Even when the request is due to pressure from outside the institution, the busy dean or personnel director may find it hard to respond.

One of the common models for organizing data for reporting is through a partnership. The institutional researcher works with programmers from a central data processing department to design a set of reporting files extracted from the live data bases. The institutional research office itself may do the reporting from these files, or it may define standardized reports for production by the data processing center. Which of these methods is chosen is likely to depend on the amount of technical expertise within the institutional research office and the tools available. If the only way to retrieve data is by use of a COBOL program, the institutional research office is unlikely to retrieve its own data, but the availability of a simple report writer or statistical software package changes things considerably. The quality and responsiveness of the data processing department also influences whether or not this model works well. This issue will be covered in more detail in the next section.

Where staff time and expertise allow, complete control of data by the institutional research office is the most versatile and efficient method to follow. With appropriate software and direct access to data bases, the institutional research office can create its own census files and build its own data bases. However, this requires considerable staff expertise and time to organize, document, and maintain. When data files are under the direct control of the institutional research office, that office must document and maintain them, as well as take responsibility for setting up and maintaining backup, security, and access procedures, functions that would otherwise fall to data custodian and data processing offices.

In summary, the first step in getting data into usable form is to move away from paper reporting. Whether to move toward complete control of data or to work with a central data processing office is a highly individual decision that depends on the mix of tools and skills available to both parties. Since it is easy to move toward more independence but not so easy to move in the other direction, investigate options thoroughly before making a final tactical plan.

**Working with Data Processing Personnel.** The relationship between the personnel in the institutional research office and those in data processing is of crucial importance to the success of the reporting function, particularly in the amount of effort needed in the initial stages of getting a reporting data base organized. There are few, if any, institutions where there is no data processing function involved in maintaining hardware, software, and administrative data, and the norm is a centralized administrative data processing function that maintains not only the hardware, software, and data bases but also the data-access processes.

While models of the data processing function are legion (Staman, 1987; Glover, 1988), there are some issues regarding data processing that are of great importance in deciding what role the institutional research office will want data processing personnel to play in reporting and how to obtain their cooperation in that role. If the only data processing resource is a traditional centralized function staffed by COBOL programmers, communication may be hard to maintain, especially if no one in the institutional research office has programming expertise, and will need a great deal of effort and good will. The result may be the need for increased expertise within the institutional research office. In a decentralized system both expertise and power is likely to be more diffused, and the relationships easier to maintain. Even in a highly centralized system, however, when there is a data administrator charged with oversight of the institutional data, this person will act as a mediating force and interaction is likely to be smoother. An information center whose job is to work with users of administrative data systems also tends to perform this function and can be useful both in training personnel and in obtaining appropriate software for access and analysis of data.

Whatever the pattern at an institution, it is imperative for the new institutional research office to put effort into making communications as smooth as possible. Without this, reporting can become unnecessarily burdensome. Some offices have decided to remove as much of their computer use as possible to a local microcomputer network because of poor relations with their computer center, only to discover that operating their own data processing function is extremely costly in personnel time and expertise. Sadly, the usual outcome is that the institutional research office does not make this discovery until the hidden time bomb explodes, because they were ignorant of the need to perform many of the tasks that are routine for systems and operations professionals. While creating a partnership with data processing staff may appear to take too much time—and sometimes it indeed does not work—it can result in an office making the best use of both centralized facilities and local options. It is worthwhile finding out what works for other offices as a guide to tactics, and it is a good idea to make sure that the data-processing personnel understand the level of expertise in the institutional research office and *vice versa*.

## Evaluating the Reporting Capability

This chapter has been concerned so far with setting up a reporting capability, but the successful institutional research office will quickly discover that many of the skills needed in the initial stages are just as important a year, or even ten years, later. A continuous evaluation of the reporting capability, including documentation and data quality control, can create a progressively improving reporting capability, whether measured in terms of accuracy or range and detail of reports. Continuous evaluation is born of the reality that one cannot check everything about every data source before beginning reporting. The institutional research office must make the decision to start somewhere and reevaluate periodically.

**Evaluating the Process.** The process whereby the institution's data are collected, entered, and maintained is one in which the institutional research office should be closely involved. One of the tenets in the search for data is never to assume that anything works exactly the way it is purported to. If you need to know at which point to create your census, or which files to use, first find out how a record enters those files. With student data, for instance, follow a record from admission to graduation, having the person who does the job explain the steps. If the registrar is trying to be courteous by explaining the process, tactfully suggest that you not waste such valuable time, and have the routine explained by the person whose daily task this is. A clerk tends to develop his or her own techniques, and those are the details you need to know.

**Evaluating the Data.** One of the most fruitful initial strategies is to find trustworthy people to work with, and then trust them. This group will expand over time as it becomes clear which departments consistently produce good data. If a department has kept its data clean for the last three semesters, it is probably wise to expend effort somewhere else and only check their data if anomalies occur. A network of trusted people is one of the most valued assets an institutional research office can have.

When evaluating data, whether investigating a new source or looking in greater depth at an old one, examine the data on the basis of the following points:

• *Presence of the data.* Are the data actually there, and if not, why not? Incorrect naming practices or accidental deletion of files can cause data to "disappear." Sometimes data are simply not entered or not transferred from other files.

• *Completeness.* Does the file contain all the records that it should? If all registered students are purported to be on a file, is this really so or do some get held back, or "administratively withdrawn," for operational reasons?

• *Quality.* Are the data coded as they should be, and how much data are missing or inconsistent?

• *External consistency.* Do the data make sense when compared with other sources? If 600 new freshmen are enrolled in classes, then 600 must have been admitted. If 250 faculty are teaching at least one course, then those 250 faculty should be accounted for in the personnel system. This external consistency should be checked across time as well as across systems. Gose (1989) provides some helpful insights on improving data quality, as do Howard, McLaughlin, and McLaughlin (1989).

It is important for this type of data checking to be ongoing, but it is hard to allocate much time to the task. Where a well-developed sense of data as an institutional resource exists, much will be accomplished by the data custodian offices or data administration, and the institutional researcher will be able to take quality control for granted. However, where this attitude does not exist, it is necessary to personally encourage a sense of responsibility for data and to educate other offices on the utility of data entry edits and routine exception reports.

Where there are no alternatives to spending time to check data, the most efficient technique is to ensure that the important data are as clear as possible before moving on to those that are less vital. The risk in attempting to check and clean all data items at once is that although the overall level of data quality may improve, important items will not be as clean as they might. It is also a good plan (and this is as true for paper records as for computerized files) to concentrate as much effort as possible on the part of the system that represents the earliest point of data entry. If student records are accurate in the admissions files, this accuracy is likely to be reflected in subsequent registration records.

## Conclusion

Reporting is not only important, it is rather like housework: as soon as one task is complete it is time to embark on another, and by the time you think that you are finished, it is time to start all over again. However, with automation and data management, the proportion of time spent on reporting, routine or ad hoc, should decline. Reporting may not be the most stimulating of jobs, but it does not need to cripple an office and prevent more interesting work from being done.

## References

Borden, V.M.H., and Delaney, E. L. "Information Support for Group Decision Making." In P. Ewell (ed.), *Enhancing Information Use in Decision Making.* New Directions for Institutional Research, no. 64. San Francisco: Jossey-Bass, 1989.

Glover, R. H. "Realizing the Benefits of Information Technology Investments on Campus." *CAUSE/EFFECT,* 1988, *11* (5), 11-16.

Gose, F. J. "Data Integrity: Why Aren't the Data Accurate?" AIR Professional File, no. 33. Tallahassee, Fla.: Association for Institutional Research, 1989.

Howard, R. D., McLaughlin, G. W., and McLaughlin, J. S. "Bridging the Gap Between the Data Base and User in a Distributed Environment." *CAUSE/EFFECT,* 1989, *12* (2), 19-25.

Staman, E. M. "Tools and Models for Computing and Communications Services." In E. M. Staman (ed.), *Managing Information in Higher Education.* New Directions for Institutional Research, no. 55. San Francisco: Jossey-Bass, 1987.

*Jennifer Wilton is associate director for data management in the office of policy research and planning, University of Massachusetts at Boston.*

*With the continually growing demand for more comprehensive, timely, and accurate data to support management decision making, institutions are turning to data administration to achieve that goal.*

# Organizing for Information Resource Management

*Karen L. Miselis*

Data management has become a difficult and perplexing problem for higher education administrators across the country, whether they are in smaller or large institutions. The growth of institutional involvement in planning, the increase in federal demands for information, and the squeeze of very tight budgets have greatly increased the demands for detailed, accurate, and comprehensive information. Institutional researchers have found it increasingly difficult to provide the required information because of the shortcomings of information management in their own institutions.

In Chapter Four Wilton describes how institutional research offices can begin to overcome common difficulties with data retrieval for institutional planning, evaluation, and reporting in mind. Often the only approach available involves monumental and extremely time-consuming work on data checking and cleanup. Senior administrators in many institutions, however, are realizing that in order to make progress in fulfilling the growing information needs of their institutions, major changes in organizational structure and direction will be needed. In this chapter I explore an organizational strategy that is taking hold in business and industry and is slowly spreading to higher education.

It is critical to understand at the outset that institutional researchers cannot solve the problem of poor data management alone. However, they can take a lead in assuring that the problem does get resolved. The solution rests in involving the whole campus in data management. The process leading to this solution is long and difficult, but when the effort succeeds, the benefits to the whole institution can be enormous. The effort must be led by the institution's senior management. That level of support is required to meet effectively the ongoing reporting, analysis, and assessment needs of institutional research and to support strategic management of the entire institution.

## Information Resource Management

As planning and management of higher education have become more sophisticated, institutional research has changed as well, specifically in the kinds of information it produces and the kinds of information support it demands. Chapters One and Three describe the scope of practice now typical of the institutional research function. The advances in computerization during the 1980s raised the level of expectation with regard to sophisticated statistical and policy analyses. Without these advances, many institutions could only hope to produce standard reports, but now institutional researchers and other analysts are expected to have timely access to accurate data from comprehensive, integrated data bases in order to address specific studies in support of academic research and education and their management. The higher level of demand for information from all areas of the institution has brought to light major problems in data integrity. And to succeed in supporting institutional decision making, the institutional researcher, as well as other analysts and managers throughout the institution, must be able to combine information easily and flexibly from a variety of different sources with confidence in the consistency of the information.

Information, like other resources of our institutions—human, financial, and physical—must be properly managed and thus requires an appropriate managerial structure. Until technologies made us aware of the power and complexity of our information resources, we had developed no such structure. It is only with the advent of more sophisticated technology for the management of information that we have recognized the need for a formal set of policies and structures to manage the quality and flow of information throughout the institution.

Many institutions across the country have begun to establish and develop an information resource management capacity with accompanying structures and policies. What follows are suggestions regarding structures and policies for successful management of information resources. How they are implemented depends to a great extent on the size, management structure, and culture of the particular institution. However, these suggestions are general enough to apply to both small and large institutions. The management of information becomes complex even in the smallest institution because of the wide variety of services supported with information.

Wide participation across the campus in establishing this new structure is essential. The office of institutional research must become deeply involved in this process for a variety of reasons. Institutional researchers understand management's needs for information, which this new structure must fulfill. They are well aware of the need for easy access to data as well as the need for timely and accurate data. As experienced users of data they should play a major role in the development of data definitions and coding structures. Finally, they regularly deal with the very complex issues of ownership, confidentiality, and maintenance of information.

## Possible Structures for Information Resource Governance

Information is an institutional resource that is developed and used campuswide and thus requires a campuswide management structure. That structure must include one individual whose sole responsibility is information resource management, the relevant institutional units reporting to that leader, and a comprehensive committee structure to provide institutionwide representation and responsibility for all the issues involving information resource management.

**The Chief Information Officer.** Just as senior officers of the institution are responsible for leadership in the management of financial or human resources, an institution needs a chief information officer (CIO) responsible for the management of its information resources. In some instances in higher education, the CIO has been the person responsible for computing or information technology. This can work satisfactorily if there is an explicit commitment to give the CIO broadened responsibility for planning and creating an entirely new administrative structure. The CIO position should be established very carefully, considering all units within the institution that are involved with the use of data in any form. The most radical change in organizational structure of the management of information resources has been to unify under the CIO academic and administrative computing, data communications, media services, planning, institutional research, and perhaps even the library. A less dramatic approach is to bring together the various functions through comprehensive, integrated planning processes within an overall institutional governance structure for information resource management. In any structure or combination of responsibilities, the CIO must have authority and responsibility for the management of at least the institutional information resources on campus.

**The Supporting Committee Structure.** The process of establishing a management structure that is without precedent in a community will require reorienting the entire community. To do this most effectively, the broad community should be involved in a comprehensive planning process for the new structure and policies (Strategic Plan . . . , 1988). An appropriate committee structure should be set up to accomplish this task. The CIO should create a campuswide information policy advisory committee that includes senior personnel with strategic planning responsibilities. This committee should plan with the CIO and review and approve the various components of the information policy and structure as they develop. The committee should recommend to the CIO and senior management the priorities for information resource management as well as the policies and procedures for designing and developing new information systems and maintaining current systems. The committee's most important role is to assure that strategic plans for information resource management are in concert with overall institutional strategic plans.

On a larger campus, the information policy advisory committee might be supplemented with an information resource managers' committee, which would undertake the more detailed work of setting priorities and reviewing policies and procedures, then making recommendations to the information policy advisory committee (Strategic Directions . . . , 1990). The membership of the managers' committee would consist of those professionals who manage information resources from across the campus, whether they work in separate schools or in central, functional offices.

**The Administrative Infrastructure.** In addition to the system of information-resources committees, there must be established an administrative infrastructure for campuswide management of information resources. Just as there may be many financial officers or business administrators who are responsible for the management of financial resources for the entire campus and building administrators who are responsible for facilities management, there must also be individuals responsible for the management of information resources for the campus as a whole. Most institutions have a central information systems unit responsible for certain aspects of the development and maintenance of centralized institutional information systems. In addition, there are often separate custodians of the various information systems who have a role to play in the administrative infrastructure. Those custodians would be, for example, the registrar for the registration system or the director of admissions for the admissions system. It is the responsibility of individual custodians to enforce the various information policies with regard to their particular system. Custodians are responsible for data access and security for their systems and must ensure that any changes made to the systems fit the institutional information architecture so that the changes do not compromise data integrity.

At the level of large units on a large, complex campus, there would probably be a person responsible solely for information management, the director of information services in the human resources office, for example. That individual should certainly be a member of one of the information planning committees. Under that individual might be several information professionals, who provide a variety of computing services to the unit. Finally, the most decentralized responsibility for the management of information resources rests in the hands of the business administrators and academic departmental assistants. These individuals are often unaware of their responsibility for the quality and timeliness of data. Departmental staff, for example, fill out forms pertaining to personnel, payroll, or course offerings. As these functions begin to include on-line data entry, it becomes vital that these staff be helped to understand their responsibilities not only for the accuracy and timeliness of those data, but for data security and appropriate use of information. For an information resource management structure to work effectively considerable training must be offered to all the individuals involved.

The individual orchestrating this organizational process for the CIO should be the institution's data administrator (Durell, 1989). This is a position that is new to higher education but is essential to the success of the information resource management effort on campus. The position has, in fact, existed for some time in private industry. In a large institution, data administration should be established as a separate office consisting of the data administrator and a small staff of data analysts. (It might also include data-base administration, which is concerned with the institutional administrative data base, or the information center, which is responsible for providing support to users of the institutional administrative data base [Durell, 1989].) In a smaller institution, the responsibility for data administration might be assumed by the institutional research office. In this circumstance, however, it is unlikely that a single person could fulfill both roles. The data administrator should manage the information planning committees, and manage the drafting and approval of the various information policy documents.

## The Role of the Institutional Data Administrator

The role of the data administrator is quite broad and varied, with specific responsibilities depending most often on the particular culture and organization of the individual institution. The fundamental role of the data administrator is to assure the accessibility, security, integrity, accuracy, and timeliness of institutional data. To do that, the data administrator must educate the community on the importance of information as an institutional resource and must establish and enforce information resource policies and standards.

The location of the data administrator within the institution is extremely important in enabling him or her to exercise appropriate authority and provide the proper level of service to the institution (Durell, 1989). The data administrator should report directly to the institution's chief information officer, if that function exists. Data administration must be independent of, though closely connected to, administrative information services, especially the office responsible for application development. It should also be connected to institutional research, since it plays an important supportive role to that activity.

The various responsibilities of the data administrator can be grouped into the following seven areas:

1. Information systems planning and data-architecture design
2. Information resource policy development and approval
3. Creation and maintenance of a data encyclopedia
4. Information security and access
5. Information system development and program management
6. Institutional awareness of information as a critical resource
7. Support of institutional research and planning.

**Information Systems Planning and Data Architecture Design.** In order to be effective the data administrator must be responsible for organizing and supporting information resource planning at a variety of levels. True progress with data integrity, accuracy, and timeliness will only come with the planning and development of new systems. There are real limitations to how much we can improve old systems. Thus, the data administrator functions as the chief planning officer for the CIO, organizing and supporting the information resource planning committee described above.

The first and most important step in information resource planning is establishing the information architecture (Curtice, 1985; Zachman, 1986). The planning and development of any new information system must have as its base a clearly defined, detailed information infrastructure. Just as the finer details of a house must be supported by a strong infrastructure, the separate information systems of any institution can have no integrity without a strong, well-defined architecture. That infrastructure is developed through an understanding of all the functions of a college or university and the relationships between them (Strategic Information . . . , 1987). The data model is then built by understanding the information entities needed to support those functions and the relationships between those entities. This data model is not connected to any technology; it is the conceptual framework which can then be used to design or modify the technological architecture of the institution.

While the data administrator must lead the effort to create an institutional data model, many members of the campus community must participate in the design of that model if it is to become a viable structure on which to build individual information systems. That participation will take place through the campus information resource planning committees.

**Information Resource Policy Development and Approval.** Just as institutions have manuals that describe policies and procedures pertaining to the management of financial resources (accounting manual) and human resources (faculty and staff handbook), so institutions need a manual on campus information policies and procedures that makes clear to the campus community the rights and responsibilities of each individual regarding the proper use of institutional information. Before describing what goes into developing such a manual, however, it is useful to define what we mean by information in general, and by institutional information in particular. A number of institutions have been tripped up by this seemingly simple task as they begin to organize for data management. In Figure 1 information is classified according to its accessibility rather than its source.

*Public-access information* is available to all members of the community, and much of the published information resides in the library. Unpublished information is that which is available through computer bulletin boards, for example. The institution has responsibility for cataloguing and protecting public-access information but is not responsible for the actual management of that information. It cannot guarantee, for example, the accuracy or timeliness of the information found in library books.

In the category of *controlled-access information,* individual information is generated and controlled by one person—a faculty member's scientific experimentation, for example, or a social scientist's survey data and analysis. When this information is stored in electronic form, the institution may be responsible for assuring the individual access to his or her data and for maintaining the privacy of those data. Work-group information might involve the generation and sharing of private information between small groups of individuals. The institution's responsibility is the same here as for individual information. *Institutional information,* which is the focus of this chapter, is generated and maintained by individuals in the academic community in the course of their work for the institution. It may be defined as information that crosses unit boundaries or is accessible to many individuals in the community, and is information for which the institution has direct management responsibility.

Under the leadership of the chief information officer, the data administrator is responsible for the drafting and approval of all policies and procedures regarding institutional information, including a general policy statement on the use and responsibilities of institutional information as well as policies and procedures on data access and security. Those documents should then be submitted for approval to the information resource

**Figure 1. Information Types by Accessibility**

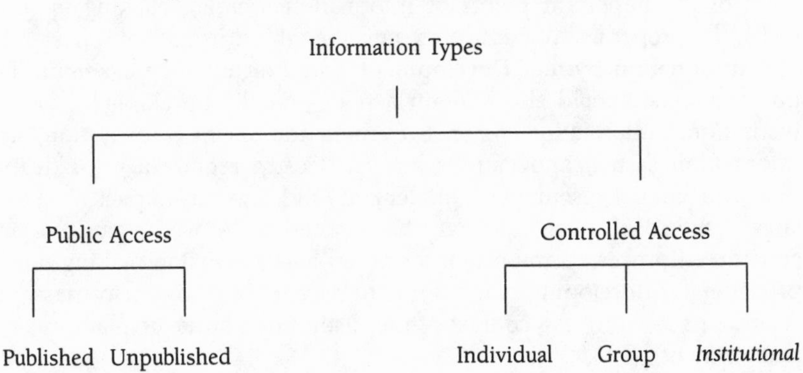

planning committees and to the campus officers. The campus information policy manual should define its sphere of responsibility regarding institutional information and should describe clearly the information responsibilities of individuals in various positions at various levels of the campus organizational structure. It should explain the importance of information as a critical institutional resource, underline the reasons each individual should use information responsibly, and describe the sanctions for violation of these policies. It should explain that institutional information cannot be owned by individual units within the institution. Individual functional units might be custodians of certain types of information and information systems, but access to and use of that information is determined by the institution.

**The Data Encyclopedia.** The information policy manual should present a policy on the creation, maintenance, and use of the campus data dictionary or encyclopedia. The major thrust of that policy should be that no new information system should be installed without a complete and comprehensive data encyclopedia. The data administrator is responsible for the creation and maintenance of the institutional data encyclopedia in order to assure its accuracy and usefulness to the community. The campus data encyclopedia contains detailed descriptions of the institutional data model, the separate institutional information systems, and every data element in the institutional data base, including the interrelationships between data elements, the time and nature of their creation, the frequency and mode of update, and the security and level of access to them (Ross, 1981). Supplemental to that data encyclopedia should be a manual for institutional research using the institution's information systems.

**Information Security and Access.** There should be a clear policy on data access and data security and a manual on data access procedures for individual systems; that is, guidelines on who has the right to access what information and how to get it. It should also include a conceptual description of the institution's data model and the various information systems that are part of it. Either this manual or separate pamphlets should inform users of the important points of information security, backing up hard disks, the proper use of passwords, and the ethical use of software.

**Information System Development and Program Management.** The policy manual should also contain a policy on the development of new institutional information systems. Even in the smallest institution, new information system applications are very costly, require a great deal of time and human resources to implement, and have an impact on a very large number of people across the institution. A well-organized and considered process is important for broad-based decision making on the priorities for developing new information systems. Those priorities must clearly be set within the context of the institution's strategic planning and management.

In addition to setting appropriate priorities regarding the development of new information systems, institutions must improve and control the management of information systems development projects if they hope to succeed in data management. Many institutions have little or no standard procedures for the development of often extremely complex information systems. Information systems projects should have wide participation across the campus and should preferably be managed by a professional in a specific functional area rather than a computing professional. Wide participation and external management require consistent standards and high-quality training. Of course, each development team should have members with expertise in data administration, institutional research, user support, data communications, application development, as well as members of the functional unit requesting the system. That team should begin its efforts with a training session in the system development process, offered by the office of data administration and supported by a comprehensive information system development project manual. The data administrator must draft and gain approval for that manual as part of the information systems planning process. At the University of Pennsylvania, the development process is called Program Management, and the Program Management manual contains not only the description of the process but also the forms to be filled in and the evaluations and decisions to be made at each step.

**Institutional Awareness of Information as a Critical Resource.** In order to assure the proper use of institutional information and information resources, the data administrator must raise the level of awareness of the institutional community that information is a critical institutional resource. This can be achieved in part through policy statements and manuals. The data administrator must reinforce this notion, however, through pamphlets, training sessions, seminars, and personal interaction. This awareness is especially important for the assurance of data integrity and accuracy when information systems are decentralized and there are literally hundreds of data input sites across the campus. Each data entry person should understand how important it is to be careful about keying in accurate, complete information.

**Support of Institutional Research and Planning.** All of the activities of the data administrator support institutional research in one way or another. The data administrator is also well positioned to provide direct support for institutional research through the development and support of an institutionwide decision support data base with easy-to-use access tools and related executive information support tools. This data base would contain relevant information obtained from all the institution's operational systems and would offer to users appropriate security, easy access, and user support in the form of a manual for institutional research and personal consulting.

## The Role of the Institutional Researcher— The First Steps

While a comprehensive information resource management system is the key to the future of quality data management, instituting and developing that system requires a major commitment from the leaders of the institution the system will serve. The institutional researcher also is essential to this process of establishing information resource management in higher education. The institutional researcher has the most comprehensive understanding of the management information needs of the institution. All of the issues of data management are very familiar to the institutional researcher.

The institutional researcher can take steps to begin to solve some initial problems and increase institutional awareness of larger problems in order to lead ultimately to the creation of a comprehensive information system. A first step that is manageable without a formal data administration capacity is to create a team of interested parties from across campus to work on developing a data dictionary for a particular system, such as human resources or student registration. As the group goes through a detailed process of agreeing on the definition of each data element in the system, the individuals will learn the intricacies and subtleties of accurate descriptions and the consequences of those subtleties for data integrity. This exercise will not only lead to a more accurately defined system, it will also help the participants to understand the necessity for a comprehensive data dictionary for the entire institution's information systems. They will also come to realize the importance of comprehensive and ongoing training for all individuals who put data into the system as well as those who use those data for analysis in support for decision making. Training is especially important as new on-line systems are installed and as data input becomes more decentralized.

A second strategy that the institutional researcher should consider is proposing the development of a decision support data base. The purpose of such a data base is to take relevant data from all the campus operational data bases in order to integrate them into a secondary data base that is for query purposes only. The query data base should be easy to use, have good facilities for various levels of security, have a comprehensive, accessible data dictionary, have an easy-to-learn and easy-to-use query language, and be supported by a manual for institutional research. The query data base must also be supported by staff who teach clients how to use it most effectively. While the design, development, and implementation of such a secondary data base requires some expertise and the allocation of some additional resources, the process will succeed in raising all the important issues involving data management at any institution. Thus it will not only provide a resource for those who need institutional data, it will also provide impetus for the more comprehensive process of planning for information resource management.

The third strategy is for the institutional researcher to continually articulate the need to establish a data administration function at the institution. The addition of just one person will begin to make a difference. The position of data administrator might be quite properly placed in institutional research as an initial step. An individual could then work full time on introducing the concepts of information resource management to the campus and might eventually succeed in initiating the establishment of a planning process for information resource management.

The most significant outcome of any one of these efforts would be for senior management to embrace information resource management as a priority for the institution and devote sufficient resources to begin the process of establishing it. Until that time, we can only continue to work valiantly to provide the information necessary for strategic decision making and to improve our institutions' information systems around the margins.

This chapter outlines a process of major proportions that will require enormous support from the institution's chief executive and years of commitment to implement. I am convinced, however, that we will never have effective data management without this process. Other, less comprehensive solutions are only temporary and imperfect. They may seem to help for a short while, but the problem will continue to worsen unless the underlying problems are attacked head on.

## Additional Resources for Data Administration

Adrian, M. "Dictionary Key to Data Access." *Computerworld,* 1986, *20* (49), 37-47.

Cortada, J. W. *Strategic Data Processing.* Englewood Cliffs, N.J.: Prentice-Hall, 1984.

Durell, W. R. *Data Administration: A Practical Guide to Successful Data Management.* New York: McGraw-Hill, 1985.

Durell, W. R. *The ABC's of Information Resource Management.* Princeton, N.J.: Data Administration, 1986.

Gillenson, M. L. *Database.* New York: Wiley, 1985.

Gillenson, M. L. "Trends in Data Administration." *MIS Quarterly,* 1985, *9* (4), 315-325.

Hawkins, B. L. (ed.). *Organizing and Managing Information Resources on Campus.* McKinney, Tex.: Academic Computing Publications, 1989.

Henderson, M. M. "The Importance of Data Administration in Information Management." *Information Management Review,* 1987, *4,* 41-47.

Holloway, S. "Data Administration in the Organization." *Data Processing,* 1986, *28* (4), 195-198.

Holloway, S. *Data Administration.* Hants, England: Gower Technical Press, 1988.

Kahn, B. K. "Some Realities of Data Administration." *Communications of the ACM,* 1983, *26* (10), 794-799.

Penrod, J., and Dolence, M. "Strategic Planning for Information Resources Management." *CAUSE/EFFECT*, 1987, *10* (3), 10–17.

*Program Management at Penn: A Manual for Participants.* Philadelphia: Office of Information Systems and Computing, University of Pennsylvania, 1989.

Ravindra, P. S. "Data Administration: An Old Function Adapts to Its New Role." *Journal of Information Systems Management*, 1986, *3* (4), 75–77.

Ravindra, P. S. "The Shared Benefits of Data Administration." *Journal of Information Systems Management*, 1987, *4* (1), 74–75.

Rockart, J. F., and Bullen, C. V. *The Rise of Managerial Computing.* Homewood, Ill.: Dow Jones-Irwin, 1986.

Shah, A. D. "Data Administration: It's Crucial." *Datamation*, 1984, *30* (1), 56–59.

Tillman, G. "Why Data Administration Fails." *Computerworld*, 1987, *21* (36), 73–76

Viskovich, F. "From Anarchy to Architecture." *Computerworld*, 1988, 22 (17), 73–77.

Wertz, C. *The Data Dictionary: Concepts and Uses.* Wellesley, Mass.: QED Information Sciences, 1986.

## References

Curtice, R. M. *Strategic Value Analysis.* Englewood Cliffs, N.J.: Prentice-Hall, 1985.

Durell, W. R. *Confessions of a Data Administrator.* Princeton, N.J.: Data Administration, 1989.

Ross, R. G. *Data Dictionaries and Data Administration.* New York: AMACOM, 1981.

*Strategic Directions for Information Systems and Computing at the University of Pennsylvania.* Philadelphia: University of Pennsylvania, 1990.

*Strategic Information Resource Management Plan of the University of Pennsylvania.* Philadelphia: University of Pennsylvania, 1987.

*Strategic Plan for Information Resources Management.* Los Angeles: California State University, 1988.

Zachman, J. A. *A Framework for Information Systems Architecture.* IBM Los Angeles Scientific Center Report, no. G320-2785. Los Angeles: IBM Los Angeles Scientific Center, 1986.

*Karen L. Miselis is associate dean for administration in the School of Arts and Sciences at The University of Pennsylvania. Prior to that, she was the University's first assistant vice-provost for data administration and information resource planning.*

*The path to quality in institutional research operations requires just seven steps and a constant attention to the ABC's of computing.*

# Selecting Appropriate Computing Tools

*William L. Tetlow*

Technology has always changed more rapidly and more radically than human beings and human organizations can accommodate easily. Therefore, the primary task of selecting computing tools for institutional research must start with some careful analysis of the institutional environment. "The more things change the more they remain the same" could well be the motto of institutional researchers around the world as they engage in the collection, analysis, and reporting of data and the transformation of those data into information.

While there have been phenomenal changes in the technology to perform these essential tasks, the fundamental institutional research activities have not changed. Data must still be collected, purified of errors and anomalies, and standardized so that aberrations are properly revealed. These data must then be analyzed, interpreted in context, and summarized and presented in a clear and concise fashion that is appropriate for the intended audience. At the same time, however, the tools available to perform these tasks are constantly changing. It is now possible to expend considerably less time and effort in all phases of institutional research, especially in the analytical reporting, and presentation phases.

At this writing, the Micro Millennium, which was predicted by Christopher Evans (1979) and described as the "transformation of world society at all kinds of levels" (p. 9) as a result of computer technology, is well established. We are witnessing the "colossal pressures that are already driving computer evolution on an upward spiral." These changes and their fundamental impact on every facet of our lives is most evident in the manner in which we perform tasks and the time and effort expended.

Much less evident are new or changed tasks that are the direct result of the technology employed.

Economists frequently measure these changes by describing how many fewer hours of labor are required to purchase common commodities such as housing, food, and transportation than were required in the past. Veteran institutional research professionals can amuse neophytes with tales of the many hours spent restoring folded, spindled, or mutilated punch cards and deciphering mysterious magnetic coding patterns on unlabeled data tapes. Equally time-consuming were the endless editorial revisions of final reports that were performed by skilled typists with normal but limited patience and good humor. Today, by contrast, it is possible for data to be processed in fractions of seconds, reports word processed and edited with minimal effort, and results sent across continents and oceans in a matter of seconds.

Since we can rest assured that the tools used to achieve institutional analyses will change constantly, it is essential that the institutional research professional always keep current with technological advances and the potential they present for improving decision making in higher education. It is imperative that one not succumb to the trap of complacency, for that is the surest path to irrelevance. To illustrate, just a few years ago an analyst in a small institution explained that the reason an available microcomputer was not being used was because "the thing is no good because it won't process my punch cards."

How then begin the process of systematically assessing the institutional research milieu and selecting the correct computing tools? It matters not whether you are establishing a formalized institutional research effort for the first time or evaluating an existing operation. Stated concisely, you must first determine the information requirements and decision-making style of the decision makers, then assess the capacity of the institution's personnel to perform or use institutional research activities, before concerning yourself with computing hardware, software, and operating systems. Often overlooked in the first phase is an examination of the organizational structures and missions of the various departments already performing some portion of institutional research.

Experiences from institutional research and computing consultancies have led to some firm convictions about the ingredients for a successful institutional research operation and, most particularly, for the appropriate computing technology. Therefore, the remainder of this chapter will consist of some prescriptions for the process that must be followed to ensure success in selecting appropriate computing tools.

## Analyze Information Requirements and Audiences

Over the course of the past twenty-five years I have had the good fortune to be involved in the creation of one pioneering institutional research office, in redirecting and reshaping the mission of another at a second university, and in resurrecting a third such office that was moribund and nearly extinct. The first was the result of a single ad hoc request from the university's board of trustees for an enrollment forecast, and the activity emphasis happened to be data collection; thus the technological tools most needed were the telephone and a calculator. The second situation was caused by a change in presidential leadership from that of a kindly, humanistic mathematician who distrusted computers and who had led the university with a paternalistic style honed over sixty years, to that of a clinical psychologist with a decided preference for data based decision making. In this case, mainframe computers of several types were used for data collection and presentations were made to the university's board of governors and other senior government officials with microcomputers controlling graphic video projectors. The third instance was precipitated by the campuswide recognition that a once-exemplary institutional research operation had been decimated by neglect to the point that essential planning data were evidently erroneous and therefore useless to the university's board of regents and to the statewide higher education coordinating commission. The computing technology employed involved data extraction from mainframe data bases, electronic transmittal into local area networks, and results distributed frequently via electronic mail.

In each case noted above, the information requirements of the decision makers were different and required emphasis on a different phase of the institutional research process. In the first instance the organizational intelligence required was internally directed and led to an emphasis on data collection. In the second case the result of several years of data collection and editing was so effective that the institutional research emphasis was on internal communications with an emphasis on data presentation. The critical component in the final case was the need to clean up erroneous data and communicate effectively with external constituencies, state and federal agencies. In each case the appropriate available computer technology was employed. In each instance, however, the computing technology used was influenced by some computing constants as well as by human and situational variables.

The task for the individual who is attempting to assess the computing tools required for institutional research therefore begins with an assessment of the situation. After a reconnaissance has been made and the results assessed, one needs to take a close look at the nature and scope of existing institutional research capacities.

## Assess the Existing Institutional Research Capacity

From the very beginning of higher education there have been decision makers who have had a desire for data based decision making. Consequently, in any existing institution there are a wide variety of individuals and departments who have collected useful data, and many who do so on a routine basis. Since there are always more analytical needs than individuals to perform institutional research tasks, it is essential to avoid duplication of effort.

First, start with those individuals who need to have a global perspective of their institution, like vice-presidents, the chief librarian, the registrar, the budget official, and so forth, in order to determine what data have been routinely collected and used in their decision making. Collect paper or electronic copies of these data bases wherever possible, but concentrate primarily on the data and information needs currently being satisfied by existing efforts so that you can focus your efforts on unmet needs.

## Assess the Existing Institutional Computing Capacity

Some institutions are blessed with an abundance of computing capacity, expert professional staff, and nearly flawless operations. If you find yourself in this paradise, quickly develop a strong and bonded relationship with those computing professionals and do everything in your power to make the institutional research connection a symbiotic one. Those less fortunate need to ascertain certain key technical parameters about the computing environment. First, determine whether your institution maintains one combined academic and administrative computing environment or has separate computers for these functions. Make sure your information is current, because almost every institution fluctuates between these two computing paradigms over time.

Second, ascertain the brand names, model numbers, operating system versions, processor memory available to any given user, and storage medium and capacity for data files on all systems with which you need to interact. Typically, you will find that you need to integrate and analyze data from two incompatible systems. Next, request copies of the system performance indices that are maintained by any well-run data processing operation. Pay particular attention to the time and duration of peak loads such as registration, course drop/adds, pre-final term papers, payroll runs, or research loads. In addition to processor loads, look very carefully at the percentage of storage capacity available at all times. Determine whether your needs will or could be impacted by these institutional constants.

At this juncture you need to decide whether the institutional research functions can be best served by requesting or augmenting dedicated resources on the centralized computing system or by extracting data sets and transporting them to a local system, either a powerful personal computer with large storage capacity or a local area institutional research network. In many cases, the preferred arrangement is a combination of all of the above. Large computing environments are organizationally designed and staffed to attend to matters such as data integrity, security, backup, and system maintenance, to name a few of the important but less visible parameters. As Wilton notes in Chapter Four, the time and effort, not to mention the cost, of these operations is always significant and not well appreciated by those who began their computing education in the personal computer era.

On the other side of the ledger, however, is the fact that some excellent software tools exist only in the personal or small computing arena. To illustrate, while the electronic spreadsheet has been credited with creating the microcomputing revolution on a worldwide basis, over ten years after its creation no large computer version of this same software exists with equivalent capability. Furthermore, almost every piece of large computer software presupposes a degree of technical computing proficiency to understand and operate that only a very few people in our society possess.

Thus, the complete institutional research operation incorporates the best of all of these modes of operation and uses each for its particular strengths while avoiding the inherent weaknesses in each.

## Create or Improve a Planning Data Base

It is axiomatic that all college and university departments, except those with an explicit planning mission, acquire and maintain only enough data to enable them to perform their operational mission. This is especially true of institutional data processing and admissions and records operations. Wilton describes in Chapter Four the problems that may be encountered when using these data. Rarely, if ever, do they maintain any kind of longitudinal or time-series data base. While many years of annual "snapshot" data may be maintained in the system, they are not edited and made consistent for the purposes of time-series analysis. It is necessary for the institutional research operation to develop and maintain its own data base which is designed for analysis and planning purposes.

By all means, however, guard against the notion that more data is better. Too often one is seduced by the opportunity to massage literally thousands of unit data records in search of the "diamond" that is buried therein. What is forgotten is that the diamond was created by a tremendous compression force and subjected to much heat in its making. Your decision makers want the "diamonds" you can produce and not the "slurry" resulting from the mining process.

## Employ Computing Experts

Just as the expertise of the Anji San, or pilot of seventeenth-century Japanese sailing vessels, was absolutely essential for a successful sea voyage, so also is the technical computer expertise of the institutional research staff essential. If there exists a successful institutional research operation without such skills on the institutional research staff, then that institution either exists in anarchy or is highly dependent on interdepartmental cooperation. All intelligence operations obtain over eighty percent of their information from publicly available information. However, it is the ability to extract data and information from a technological potpourri, to blend and synthesize data from diverse sources, that marks a successful institutional research operation. Institutional research technical staff are frequently the only computer specialists in the institution that have to cope with nearly every type of hardware and operating system in use at an institution; in some cases, they must deal with technical issues outside the institution. They are the ones who extract essential data from different technical media to record in a third medium best suited for planning and analysis.

It is also essential that these specialists be part of the institutional research staff because every operation that attempts to use centralized data processing staff experiences incorrect and misleading data or suffers from terminal cases of priority queuing.

If technical institutional research staff do not exist or do not have the necessary breadth of skills to enable them to assess other computing resources in the institution, one should then engage a consultant who does possess both institutional research and computing experience. What is essential is that you have an individual who can assess the operation from a data perspective rather than from a purely technical computing perspective. To illustrate, at one institution I discovered that there were three valid codes for a mainframe data-base field that was labelled "Sex." Since I was unaware that the Almighty had created anything other than males and females, and since I believed that the field was unlikely to have the values "yes, no, and maybe" encoded in that data-base area, I requested an elaboration of the valid entries. To my surprise I discovered that the entries stood for "Mr., Mrs., and Miss." This field had obviously been established by a computer technician who had commingled a gender field and a title field and had only come up with three values; inexplicably absent were "Dr., Ms., Col.," and so on. However, it was equally apparent that the field had been established to meet a particular limited function, such as preparing general mailing labels, and had not been assessed for its potential contribution to the institutional research effort.

## Determine Your Software Needs

Every computing professional will tell you to determine your requirements before selecting your software, then to select your operating system based on the required software, and lastly to select your hardware. This advice is as sound today as it was thirty or more years ago. One will find, however, that there may be more useful software tools for institutional research purposes in the personal or small-computer area than is true in the large-computer collection. Examine your needs in word processing, desktop publishing, analytical or statistical analysis (including spreadsheet style), graphics, communications, and data base applications. Select only those products that are widely used or supported in your area (including the local community), unless you have special needs. You will find that these products are usually those that have the best documentation, third-party manuals and training guides, user groups for assistance and advice, vendor support, and have exhibited "staying power" as a result of product excellence plus well-managed and well-capitalized companies. In this regard, one vendor in particular, Microsoft, is especially well positioned for market dominance in the nineties because it has a wide variety of software that runs on a wide variety of small-computer hardware platforms.

## Obtain Sufficient Resources for Independent Operations

Every institutional research operation I have been associated with or observed that has a reputation for excellence has the capability to operate independently from other computing and analytical resources. This translates, today, into having dedicated hardware resources for institutional research data bases, and software and human resources that need not be shared with other operations. Institutional research often operates in a time frame that cannot tolerate priority queuing for hardware, software, or human resources. In addition, there needs to be a physical separation to safeguard against accidental, unauthorized, or untimely access to analysts and computing resources. At one institution the annual "snapshot" data tapes were placed in the pool and accidentally overwritten by operations personnel of the computing center to meet an operation crisis. A second copy of the key data kept in a second location is just as absolute a requirement as cross-training of key personnel.

The hardware to accomplish this in even the largest institution can be obtained for as little as $10,000 in 1990. Some smaller institutions could operate on as little as $5,000. A third-generation desktop computer, on benchmark tests rated from at least twenty to forty times faster than the original IBM personal computer, can be obtained for that sum. Such a computer can perform from five to twenty million computing instructions per second (5-20 MIPS), has a storage capacity of from one-hundred to three-hundred million characters or numbers (100-300 Mb), can display graphs and photographs with a resolution that rivals photography (1,024 × 768 pixel resolution), and can be obtained at an education discount for $10,000 or less.

I am presently using such a machine in my own work. Its educational institution cost was less than $5,000. It has a working memory of 4 million characters (4 Mb RAM), a fixed-disk storage capacity of 120 million characters (120 Mb), and a graphic resolution of 640 × 480 pixels (VGA standard). For less than an additional $2,000, the graphic resolution could be increased to the levels mentioned above or more. A further $1,500 buys storage capacity with removable disc packs, which hold 44 Mb each. The last $1,500 of the $10,000 budget could be spent for a laser printer with a resolution approximating 400 dots per inch. This machine has a benchmark computing test rating that is twenty-one times that of the IBM PC XT and a hard disk speed rating that is ten times as fast.

Removable archival storage devices that use either magnetic or optical media can be obtained for around $1,000. Laser printers that can print text, graphs, and charts at 300 dots per inch resolution or more cost only $1,000 to $3,000. Color laser printers are available for less than $10,000. Scanners to convert images to computer manipulable code are only $1,000. Ten years ago such a machine would have cost several million dollars. My machine weighs less than twenty pounds and is the size of an executive briefcase.

For those with an outstanding centralized computing environment a similar investment in dedicated hardware and software purchases can achieve the same effect. A dedicated computer with dedicated storage can be located in a centralized environment where it can be attended and maintained by central operations staff, thus freeing the institutional research staff from these onerous but absolutely essential tasks.

Since computing hardware and software costs have decreased steadily and regularly over the entire history of computing, we can reasonably expect these costs to look ridiculously high in only a few years. Most importantly, the hardware and software required to follow this prescription will cost less than the salary and benefits of the lowest paid full-time analyst on the institutional research staff.

Transferring information and data from one hardware platform (or machine) to another has been a vexing task because, until now, all the incentives were to keep solutions and operations as proprietary as possible. The marketplace is changing, however, and "interconnectivity," or the ease with which dissimilar machines can be interconnected, is the current buzzword. There are no easy solutions, but there is one prescription to make your task as nearly painless as possible. Try to arrange to have your data "exported" from its source program in the most common coding convention in the world today, American Standard Code for Information Interchange (ASCII). If your data or text has been reduced to this common standard, it can be transported more easily from one environment to another.

When following the seven prescriptions described above for selecting the appropriate computing tools, always remember the following ABC's:

*A. Acquire and Maintain Quality in Everything.* Only quality tools should be employed because it always costs more, in rework and recovery costs, to rectify problems caused by inferior equipment or programs than it would have cost to acquire quality hardware and software in the first instance. In addition, the time expended searching for solutions because of inadequate or nonexistent documentation, inadequate software, or hardware limitations can consume as much as 50 percent of valuable and scarce human resources. Finally, hiring trainees rather than more experienced, and admittedly more costly, staff always results in poor productivity and large, although often unmet, training needs.

*B. Buy the Best Available Information Technology Your Budget Permits.* As heretical as it might sound to those employed in nonprofit institutions, always buy the most computing power and the best available technology that your budget will permit. The evolutionary growth rate is accelerating exponentially, and manufacturers are now releasing new, more powerful computer models every few months. The best and newest applications software requires more hardware capability than ever before and will not function on older more limited equipment. By buying at or near the top of the manufacturer's line you increase the effective useful life of your hardware; current wisdom suggests three to five years of effective useful hardware life before it is technologically obsolete. Furthermore, it is not unusual for educational capital budget infusions to occur only every five or more years; you might have to live with your equipment long past its prime before you can obtain funds for replacement.

For software the same advice is often but not always true. Although by buying the latest version of a software package you may gain functionality that you may not need at the outset, you may also be burdened with longer learning and training times as a direct result of the package's increased capability. As a rule, though, one should not buy a version 4.xx when a version 5.xx is being marketed unless one is merely waiting for the new release deficiencies to be remedied.

This does not always mean the most expensive option is the best, however, because many excellent alternatives are available. The best communications package I have used cost thirty-five dollars and was marketed by a distribution scheme called "shareware" whereby owners were legally encouraged to share their copies with other users and then, after trial use, to legally register their copies. My father used to advise me to carefully consider the next-to-the-top-priced option when buying because thus I would often get the functionality I needed without unnecessary and highly priced "frills." Be a careful consumer and demand value for your dollar.

Whenever I am asked how to find out what is the best technology for the intended application I always respond with a strategy rather than a specific recommendation. First, identify five to ten acknowledged experts in the domain in question. Then ask them to name the three best options in the area in question. Also ask them to name the three best publications that contain objective descriptive and preferably evaluative reviews. Finally, ask them for the names of local user groups, local and national bulletin boards, and electronic forums where you can find the kind of detailed information that you seek. What you will discover is that your search for information will soon become focused and that a consensus will emerge from all of your various sources. By then, you will often have a choice between a couple of excellent products and can select the one that provides the best match for your needs. I have used this approach to buy computers, microwave ovens, skis, and most recently, a serger for my wife; three months ago I could not even spell the word "serger" properly!

*C. Cover Your Exposure and Always Have Alternatives.* Use a strategy of redundancy to ensure that essential information is not lost permanently due to electrical or mechanical failure or to human error. This means duplicating critical data sets, storage locations, processing equipment, and trained operators. The reliability of computers has been so great in recent years that people lose sight of the fact that computers are machines, and machines eventually fail. Having a second processor, or backup data set, or even an alternate human operator will eventually repay the organization for the marginal extra cost. Failure to do so will eventually lead to a crisis.

## Summary

Selecting appropriate computing tools for performing institutional research requires an analytical strategy that is ongoing and affected by the constant changes in information technology. One must always begin, however, by assessing the informational needs and style of the key decision makers. Then a careful assessment must be made of both the existing institutional research and existing computing capacity at the institution. With that evaluation in hand, one needs to augment or create a data base specifically designed for longitudinal analysis and employ computing experts to assist in this process. Only then is it desirable to determine the software requirements and begin the process of obtaining sufficient resources to permit the institutional research group to function in a fashion independent from all other operational departments.

When following these prescriptions for selecting computing resources always pay attention to the computing ABC's: Acquire quality in everything, Buy the best that your budget will permit, and Cover your exposure by insisting on redundancy and alternative solutions for all key operations.

## Reference

Evans, C. *The Micro Millennium.* New York: Viking, 1979.

*William L. Tetlow is an independent computer applications consultant who is currently resident consultant and manager of the Demonstration and Information Center on Small Computers (DISC) at the University of Colorado, Boulder. He is past president of the Association for Institutional Research.*

*The higher education movement most likely to affect institutional research in the immediate future is the implementation of outcomes assessment across the country.*

# Organizing for Assessment

*James O. Nichols, Lori A. Wolff*

The higher education movement most likely to affect institutional research in the immediate future is the implementation of outcomes assessment across the country. It is important to understand the background of this movement in order to organize support for its implementation on each campus.

The current assessment movement began in the early 1980s with the publication of four key studies: *To Strengthen Quality in Higher Education: Summary Recommendations of the National Commission on Higher Education Issues* (1982); *A Nation at Risk: The Imperative for Educational Reform* (Bennett, 1983); *To Reclaim a Legacy: A Report on the Humanities in Higher Education* (Bennett, 1984); and *Involvement in Learning: Realizing the Potential of American Higher Education* (National Institute of Education, 1984).

In each case, these national reports called for the improvement of undergraduate education and, at the same time, an assessment of student learning. By the mid 1980s, the call for an assessment of educational accomplishments, originally placed in the context of overall improvement in undergraduate higher education, had become a separate initiative as the centerpiece for the federal government's higher education policy under Secretary of Education William Bennett. Addressing the American Council on Education in 1985, Bennett said, "Colleges should state their goals, measure their success in meeting those goals, and make the results available to everyone. . . . If institutions don't assess their own performance, others—either states or commercial outfits—will most likely do it" (Bennett, 1985, p. 25). This federal emphasis on assessment by Secretary Bennett culminated in July 1988 with a change in the federal regulations through which the government recognizes the Council on Postsecondary

Accreditation (COPA). The crux of that change in accreditation policy is as follows:

> Part 602—Secretary [of Education]'s Procedures and Criteria for Recognition of Accrediting Agencies 602.17—Focus on Educational Effectiveness
>
> The secretary determines whether [or not] an accrediting agency, in making its accrediting decisions, systematically obtains and considers substantial and accurate information on the educational effectiveness of Postsecondary Educational Institutions or Programs, especially as measured by student achievement, by—
>
> (A) Determining whether [or not] an Educational Institution or Program maintains clearly specified educational objectives consistent with its mission . . . ;
>
> (B) Verifying . . . satisfaction of Certificate and Degree requirements by all students . . . who have demonstrated educational achievement as assessed and documented through appropriate measures;
>
> (C) Determining that institutions or programs document the educational achievements of their students . . . in verifiable and consistent ways, such as evaluation of senior theses, review of student portfolios, general educational assessments (for example, standardized test results), graduate or professional school test results, graduate or professional school placements, job placement rates, licensing examination results, employer evaluations, and other recognized measures;
>
> (D) Determining the extent to which institutions or programs systematically apply the information obtained through the measures described in Paragraph (C) of this section to foster enhanced student achievement [Federal Register, 1987, pp. 25088–25099].

The higher education community responded to the early calls for assessment at the national and regional levels through their institutional and professional accreditation groups, a voluntary quality-assurance system that is unique to the United States. At the national level, the Council on Postsecondary Accreditation (1986), which recognizes both regional and professional accrediting associations across the country, stated that educational institutions and programs should sharpen statements of mission and objectives to identify intended educational outcomes, to develop additional effective means of assessing learning outcomes and results, and to use the self-evaluation in the peer-review process of accreditation as an integral part of ongoing planning and institutional programmatic change.

Among the regional accrediting associations, the Southern Association of Colleges and Schools (SACS) clearly assumed leadership in implementing outcomes assessment. In 1985, SACS made substantive changes in its *Criteria for Accreditation.* These changes stated that institutions have an obligation to all constituents to evaluate effectiveness and to use the

results in a broad-based, continuous planning anc
and that institutions must establish adequate procedu
evaluation and describe how the achievement of t
ascertained (Southern Association of Colleges and Sc

Further, SACS published a *Resource Manual on Ins*
(1987) that provided a more complete description of
its institutions, and has held its institutions accountabl
outcomes assessment. Within the other regional accrediting bodies, the notion of outcomes assessment has been treated in a less rigorous manner. Virtually all the other regional accrediting associations have had statements relating to institutional effectiveness or outcomes assessment in their "Criteria and Guidelines" for a number of years. However, in regional institutional accrediting associations other than SACS, these injunctions were enforced less rigorously until the late 1980s. The professional accrediting associations have also integrated the notion of outcomes assessment into their criteria for recognition of individual academic programs. One professional accrediting association, the American Assembly of Collegiate Schools of Business, has even gone so far as to publish its own cognitive instruments and evaluative criteria for use with individual students ("Ten-Year Effort . . . ," 1987).

At the state level, the majority of legislatures across the country have taken one action or another related to assessment in higher education (Boyer and others, 1987). These range widely from requirements that institutions describe how assessment is being conducted on their campuses (see Virginia's approach; Virginia General Assembly, 1987) to much more prescriptive requirements directing that certain assessment procedures take place on all campuses receiving public support (see South Carolina's approach; South Carolina Commission on Higher Education, 1989).

The action on individual campuses across the country has grown rapidly during the period 1987–1989. Elaine El-Khawas stated that almost seven in ten college and university chief executive officers or chief academic officers reported some assessment activity currently under way and that nearly eight in ten colleges and universities will introduce some form of comprehensive assessment program soon (1989). Table 1 illustrates the types of assessment activities reported in El-Khawas's most recent survey of chief executive and chief academic officers.

This background is important for campuses considering outcomes assessment, since it is essential that they identify the reasons for implementation prior to organizing for its accomplishment. Is the impetus for implementation regional accreditation, professional accreditation, a state mandate, or the good intentions (without external coercion) of local administrators and faculty? The answer to this question has substantive implications for institutional action.

If implementation is to satisfy local desires or intrinsic needs for

**ble 1. Status of Assessment Activities at Institutions in 1989**

| *Assessment Activities Regarding* | *Percentage in Place* | *Percentage with Action Planned* |
|---|---|---|
| Basic college-level skills | 65 | 19 |
| Knowledge in general education | 25 | 36 |
| Knowledge in major | 26 | 31 |
| Higher-order skills | | |
| Critical thinking | 14 | 46 |
| Quantitative problem solving | 18 | 42 |
| Oral communication | 21 | 39 |
| Writing | 47 | 27 |
| Changes in student attitudes and values | 17 | 34 |
| Long-term outcomes of graduates | 25 | 44 |

the information, then the institution is free to design the process that best serves its own needs. Regrettably, this is not the most common circumstance.

If the mandate for implementation is to show "Institutional Effectiveness," assessment at the departmental or program level will need to be linked with a functional statement of institutional purpose and encompass support units as well as instructional departments. On the other hand, should the institution be responding to a state-level mandate, the only requirement may be the implementation of certain student outcomes measurements.

Regardless of the individual circumstances of the institution, the first step in organizing for assessment is to determine the requirements and limiting factors imposed by external and internal forces. Then the institution can establish the relative importance of institutional effectiveness and outcomes assessment activities within the total workload of the institutional research unit.

It is important that the senior institutional research officer and his or her supervisor reach an understanding regarding the relative importance of the various tasks assigned to the institutional research unit. Several studies, including one we completed for the Georgia Board of Regents Institutional Research Officers in 1989 (Nichols and Wolff), note that a substantial difference of opinion frequently exists between the institutional research officer and his or her supervisor on task priorities. As assessment or institutional effectiveness operations are initiated, it is vital that the institutional research unit receive guidance concerning the importance of those operations within the total work of the unit.

In general, assessment or institutional effectiveness operations are a "second-level" function. That is to say, a certain amount of basic descriptive data concerning institutional operations must be in existence prior to launching an assessment effort. Failure to recognize this "second-level" nature of assessment or institutional effectiveness support activities leads some institutions to invest substantially in this endeavor only to find their efforts undermined by the lack of basic descriptive institutional research concerning campus operations.

Having decided on the reasons for undertaking institutional effectiveness or outcomes assessment and its relative importance, campus officials need to determine the resources necessary to support implementation. Many institutional research units will find it necessary to augment existing expertise as well as clerical support.

Most institutional research units are staffed by generalists from a variety of disciplines, by statisticians (occasionally with an educational research background), and by computer-related support personnel. However, in most cases, institutional research units lack staff with expertise in cognitive testing and survey research, and such expertise is often needed for outcomes assessment.

Expansion of the clerical staff to support assessment is also very likely. An institution must decide whether it will place the burden for logistical support and design of the attitudinal surveys (such as surveys of students, graduates, alumni, and employers) on the individual departmental faculty or centralize it within the institutional research unit. Many institutions find the latter more cost effective, as it does not cause a dependence on already overburdened faculty. Under such circumstances, additional clerical support is generally required. Furthermore, the institutional research unit's supplies and services budget will need to increase.

Next the institution needs to consider the organizational implications of institutional effectiveness or outcomes assessment. If the institution is implementing a comprehensive program of institutional effectiveness, including planning and assessment activities in all academic and administrative departments, then there is merit in aligning the institutional research unit under the chief executive officer. On the other hand, if the institution takes a student-outcomes orientation only, there is considerable merit in a direct organizational relationship between the institutional research unit and the chief academic officer.

Ewell and Lisensky (1988) identified a reluctance on the part of many faculties to work with existing institutional research units, which they perceive as part of the "administrative bureaucracy." On the other hand, institutional research units that are perceived as part of the academic community because they report to the chief academic officer are more likely to enjoy a close working relationship with the faculty in student-outcomes assessment.

Implementing institutional effectiveness or outcomes assessment through the expansion of an existing institutional research unit differs from establishing a new institutional research unit with the expressed focus of implementing such activities. The following sections describe each of the two situations.

## Undertaking Institutional Effectiveness and Outcomes Assessment Activities Through an Existing IR Unit

Substantive advantages, as well as disadvantages, accompany the implementation of institutional effectiveness operations by an existing institutional research unit on a campus. In this case, it is especially important to establish a clear understanding of the relative priority of assessment and institutional effectiveness operations within the overall functions of the unit.

Prior functions of an institutional research unit, such as coordination of external reporting and support of process-oriented decisions such as budgeting, do not usually cease when assessment begins. The senior institutional research officer needs to establish an understanding with his or her supervisor regarding the relative importance of assessment on the campus and the additional work involved in supporting this effort. Senior administrators tend to assume that the institutional research component can "absorb" this function among its other duties without additional resources. The assumption is apparently based on the belief that the institutional research unit currently is not fully committed and that the existing staff has the necessary proficiency in the area of assessment. The senior institutional research officer and supervisor should address both of these assumptions and either deemphasize some of the unit's existing operations or obtain additional resources.

Assigning the assessment or institutional effectiveness function to the institutional research unit may have important organizational implications. We have already noted that the nature of assessment is related to the choice of supervisor for institutional research. In addition, the level and nature of institutional research's constituencies often change. Prior to assignment of the institutional effectiveness or outcomes assessment responsibility, institutional research services may have functioned at the vice-presidential and dean levels. Subsequently, the focus of institutional research services may extend to the departmental and program level. The institutional research unit will be dealing with a greatly expanded number of constituents, many of them relatively uninformed, who may create new demands for information from the institutional research unit.

Adding assessment and institutional effectiveness as a function to an existing institutional research unit has a number of advantages. Among those advantages are

- *Building on basic institutional descriptive data.* As previously described, assessment activities represent a "second level" of institutional research activity on a campus. By adding the assessment function to an ongoing institutional research unit, one can assume that this base of information concerning campus operations is already in place.

• *The existence of an institutional research unit structure.* This advantage assumes that an existing unit structure, including supervisory skills, clerical support, and files, are already in place. Hence, adding the necessary expertise in test and measurement and survey research at the assistant director, or professional staff, level will be feasible and less costly than if a director is required. Furthermore, having an office support structure will greatly ease implementation of assessment operations.

• *Integration of assessment or institutional effectiveness services into an inventory of ongoing activities.* The academic enterprise does not accept change easily. The ability to assign assessment to an existing array of institutional research services reduces the visibility of the change and may, in many cases, make assessment more acceptable to the faculty.

Each of these advantages results from having an existing umbrella of services and a support structure into which assessment activities can be integrated as a natural development.

Unfortunately, integrating assessment activities into an existing institutional research component also carries a number of disadvantages:

• *The existing perception of the institutional research unit.* If the institutional research unit is perceived as primarily administrative in nature, providing data to off-campus sources and centralized support for administrative decision making, then its acceptance as a "legitimate" academic-support unit by the faculty will be much more difficult.

• *Responsibility without resources.* As indicated above, institutions tend to assign responsibility to an existing institutional research unit without providing the necessary resources or understanding the current workload of the unit. The result frequently is the neglect of existing institutional research services in order to accomplish the newly assigned assessment priority.

• *The notion that "anybody can do assessment."* While most assessment activities are relatively straightforward and do not require an excess of technical expertise, minimum competencies in testing, measurement, and survey research must exist in the institutional research unit, or be available through the faculty or other means. Unfortunately, this is often not the case within existing institutional research units, especially on relatively small campuses.

In summary, adding assessment to an existing institutional research unit benefits and suffers from the factors described above. On balance however, integrating assessment support operations into an ongoing institutional research unit can be accomplished at a lower cost than establishing a new institutional research unit.

## Establishment of a New Institutional Research Unit for Assessment and Institutional Effectiveness Support

Many two-year colleges and regional four-year institutions, particularly in the southern portion of the United States, have established entirely new units to implement institutional effectiveness or outcomes assessment. Spurred by the SACS *Criteria for Accreditation* (1985), this phenomenon has been described as the institutional research "Full Employment Act."

Among the advantages enjoyed by a new institutional research unit dedicated primarily to assessment support activities are the following:

- *Establishing a clear focus.* The founding of an institutional research unit to support assessment clearly solves the problem of relative priorities. This commitment should be widely disseminated on the campus so that there is no misunderstanding regarding the role of the unit.
- *Starting with a clean slate.* As a new unit, there is no "baggage" concerning perceptions of preexisting office functions with which to deal. This probably enhances the unit's acceptability to the faculty, as well as precluding an erosion of prior services.
- *Organizational relationship to the chief academic officer.* The institution focusing only on student outcomes can establish a reporting relationship between institutional research and the chief academic officer at the outset, avoiding the potentially threatening realignment of the unit's reporting relationships. If the unit is charged with support of assessing institutional effectiveness, the institution can establish an organizational structure with access to the chief executive officer.
- *Hiring the best-equipped person to handle assessment.* The absence of a previous institutional research unit requires the appointment of a management-level professional to head the unit, as well as to provide the necessary expertise in test and measurement and survey research. While this arrangement is certainly more costly than the employment of an assistant director for assessment, the ability to utilize the greater salary available for a management-level individual will enhance the degree of experience and expertise the institution can purchase.

Coupled with these advantages are a number of relative disadvantages of establishing a new institutional research unit focused primarily on assessment support services:

- *Lost economy of scale.* New units for institutional effectiveness or outcomes assessment tend to be smaller and located in relatively modest-sized institutions. The advantages of a larger unit to which assessment is an additional duty are lost, and the per-unit cost of assessment support is increased.
- *Absence of unit structure.* While the primary focus of a newly established institutional research unit may well be on assessment, a major portion of its attention, particularly in the first six months to a year, will be on

the mechanics of establishing an office structure. At least at the outset, this necessary task significantly reduces the amount of support available for the assessment process.

• *Lack of basic institutional data.* As indicated earlier, assessment support activities are primarily "second-level" activities that require institutional data on academic operations. Many new institutional research units do not have basic institutional descriptive data. Thus, the unit will need to dedicate considerable time to building a foundation of institutional information.

Establishing an institutional research unit is an exciting event accompanied by great expectations. Unfortunately, the first year of accomplishments regarding assessment support activities may be disappointing due to the need to establish a basic office structure and to gather base-level data on academic operations. Senior-level administrators need to understand this so that expectations during the first year of the unit's operations are not inflated.

## Steps in Organizing for Assessment and Institutional Effectiveness Support Operations

Whether assessment is based in a new or an existing institutional research unit, these general steps should be followed.

**Determining the Charge.** The exact requirements for assessment activities may vary substantially from institution to institution. At the outset, the senior institutional research officer should ascertain the following:

• What requirement has been placed on the institution to cause it to initiate institutional effectiveness or outcomes-assessment operations?

• What role within the institution has been delegated to the institutional research unit? To provide leadership at the policy level? To provide technical support? To provide logistical support?

Whatever the answers to these questions, the institutional research unit and the organizational unit to which it reports need a clear understanding on these matters.

**Marshalling the Resources for Implementation.** In the next step, the institutional research unit begins to identify the resources it needs to accomplish the task. If it is charged with policy-level assessment of institutional effectiveness, then additional proficiency in planning and other general administrative skills may be necessary as well as other requirements, such as the strengthening of resources in test and measurement and survey research. In conjunction with establishing staffing needs, the institution should identify resources available on the campus, such as faculty members with useful expertise on existing assessment procedures. Prior to any statement of resource requirements, the senior institutional research officer should seek to match ideal needs, existing resources, and the institution's fiscal circumstances.

**Designing the Assessment Process.** Peter Ewell's well-known statement that assessment should not attempt to "measure everything that moves" (Nichols, 1989) is particularly important in designing the assessment process. No institution possesses sufficient resources for an absolutely comprehensive assessment procedure of all academic operations. The institution's assessment procedures should be built around the statements of expected results or outcomes developed by the departments and degree programs. In so doing, the institution's assessment process will focus on what needs to be measured, as opposed to what can easily be measured, or what is already measured.

It is important to understand that the design of the assessment process is a cooperative arrangement between the institutional research unit and the faculty in each department and academic program. What should evolve is a dynamic relationship between each of the institution's academic programs and departments charged with identification of their expected results or outcomes and that group on campus (primarily the institutional research unit) charged with assessment of the extent to which these expected results or outcomes are accomplished. In most cases, a compromise is inevitable between the ideal, which may be impossible to measure, and expected results of less importance (but that are perhaps more easily measured). This compromise should shape a feasible plan for assessment built on the expected results identified by the academic departments or programs.

In the design of the assessment process, mechanisms to feed back information to the academic departments should be carefully considered. In this regard, someone will need to determine the role of the institutional research unit as a potential clearinghouse for all information on assessment. The more institutional research is able to customize its reports on assessment results, the more likely it is that the faculty will use the information. In some cases, individual presentations to academic departments will undoubtedly be the best method to ensure that this message is delivered.

**Initial Implementation.** Ideally, the institution will have the time to pilot-test individual portions of assessment, one after another. Unfortunately, this is a rare luxury in the implementation of assessment support activities. More likely, institutions must move quickly, attempting a full-scale implementation in a short time. Such an implementation will more resemble the proverbial "Chinese fire drill" than an orderly assessment procedure. The institutional research unit should expect gaps in assessment coverage, as well as problems in implementing procedures that seemed feasible during the design of the process. It is more important for the institution to persist in its assessment procedures than for the initial implementation to be smooth and efficient. Frankly, the institutional research unit can expect to muddle through the beginning stages, improving both effectiveness and efficiency in the second iteration.

short page

## Concluding Remarks

As of this writing, the federal government is seriously considering incorporating institutional effectiveness and outcomes assessment into the reauthorization of the Higher Education Act in 1991 (Hanes, 1989). Should this transpire, more institutional research units will find themselves committed to institutional effectiveness and outcomes assessment. While this effort does not constitute a new day for institutional research as a field, it does represent a substantive and apparently enduring addition to the inventory of services that institutional research provides to the higher education community.

## References

"Bennett Calls in Colleges to Assess Their Own Performance, Publish Results." *Chronicle of Higher Education*, November 6, 1985, p. 25.

Bennett, W. *A Nation at Risk: The Imperative for Educational Reform.* Washington, D.C.: United States Government Printing Office, 1983.

Bennett, W. *To Reclaim a Legacy: A Report on the Humanities in Higher Education.* Washington, D.C.: United States Government Printing Office, 1984.

Boyer, C. M., Ewell, P. T., Finney, J. E., and Mingle, J. R. *Assessment and Outcomes Measurement—A View from the States: Highlights of a New ECS Survey and Individual State Profiles.* Report PS-87-1. Denver, Colo.: Education Commission of the States, 1987.

Council on Postsecondary Accreditation. *Educational Quality and Accreditation: A Call for Diversity, Continuity, and Innovation.* Washington, D.C.: Council on Postsecondary Accreditation, 1986.

El-Khawas, E. *Campus Trends, 1989.* Higher Education Panel Report, no. 78. Washington, D.C.: American Council on Education, 1989.

Ewell, P., and Lisensky, R. P. *Assessing Institutional Effectiveness—Redirecting the Self-Study Process.* Washington, D.C.: The Consortium for the Advancement of Private Higher Education, 1988.

Federal Register, Department of Education. *34CFR Parts 602 and 603, Secretary's Procedures and Criteria for Recognition of Accrediting Agencies; Notice of Proposed Rule Making.* Washington, D.C.: Government Printing Office, 1987.

Hanes, L. L., Assistant Secretary, Office of Postsecondary Education, United States Department of Education. Remarks at Meeting of Southern Association of Colleges and Schools, Atlanta, December 10-13, 1989.

National Commission on Higher Education Issues. *To Strengthen Quality in Higher Education: Summary Recommendations of the National Commission on Higher Education Issues.* Washington, D.C.: United States Government Printing Office, 1982.

National Institute of Education, Study Group on Excellence in American Higher Education. *Involvement in Learning: Realizing the Potential of American Higher Education.* Washington, D.C.: United States Government Printing Office, 1984.

Nichols, J. O. *Institutional Effectiveness and Outcomes Assessment Implementation on Campus: A Practitioner's Handbook.* New York: Agathon Press, 1989.

Nichols, J. O., and Wolff, L. A. *Georgia System Institutional Research Survey for the Georgia Board of Regents Institutional Research Officers.* Oxford: Office of University Planning and Institutional Research, University of Mississippi, 1989.

*Resource Manual on Institutional Effectiveness.* Atlanta, Ga.: Commission on Colleges of the Southern Association of Colleges and Schools, 1987.
South Carolina Commission on Higher Education. *Guidelines for Institutional Effectiveness.* Columbia: South Carolina Commission on Higher Education, 1989.
Southern Association of Colleges and Schools. *Criteria for Accreditation: Commission on Colleges.* Atlanta, Ga.: Southern Association of Colleges and Schools, 1986.
"Ten-Year Effort Produces Outcomes Measurement Tools." *American Assembly of Collegiate Schools of Business Newsline,* 1987, 5, 2.
Virginia General Assembly. *Senate Joint Resolution 125.* Richmond: Virginia General Assembly, 1987.

*James O. Nichols is director of university planning and institutional research at the University of Mississippi.*

*Lori A. Wolff is institutional research associate in university planning and institutional research at the University of Mississippi.*

*Without viable integration strategies, the institutional researcher and the decision maker remain isolated from each other, to the ultimate disadvantage of the institution.*

# Integrating Institutional Research into the Organization

*Felice D. Billups, Lenore A. DeLucia*

Integrating the work of the institutional research office into the fabric of the higher education organization is a critical challenge for newcomers as well as for established veterans. Even the most experienced institutional researcher may occasionally overlook the basic need to link research results with decision-making processes and various campus constituencies. This chapter reviews the changing role of the institutional research office in a dynamic higher education environment, asserts the importance of integration into that environment, and outlines practical strategies for effective and successful integration of the institutional research function into the organization.

## Institutional Research in Context

The role of the institutional research office should be a critical element in the decision making of a college or university. Peterson (1985, p. 5) describes institutional research as a "critical intermediary function that links the educational, managerial, and information functions of higher education institutions. . . ." Saupe (1990) stresses the importance of internal data gathering and analysis to the successful management of colleges and universities. Similarly, Ridge (1978) identifies the job of institutional research as providing top-level information to key internal and external decision makers. While these definitions focus on the central purpose of institutional research, Dressel (1972, p. 49) reminds us that the institutional researcher's "ultimate success depends less on the research findings than on the promotion of action. . . ." If institutional research is central to the functioning of an organization, what is the best course of action to ensure effective integration of institutional research into the college setting?

Changes in higher education have created significant changes in the institutional researcher's role. Societal changes, especially those associated with the impact of shifting demographics on enrollments and of decreasing financial support for institutions and students, suggest both opportunities and limitations for higher education in the years ahead. The long-term success of an institutional research office depends on its ability to communicate those changes to the college community and to assist decision makers as they accommodate to the changes. The institutional researcher therefore must create and maintain a vital connection with the decision makers at the institution.

## Institutional Researcher as Information Activist

A successful institutional research office has moved from the passive role of information resource to that of information activist. The researcher has a responsibility to contribute as a change agent and not just as a data gatherer and analyst. Maassen (1986) summarizes the basic activities of the institutional researcher to include (1) collecting data about the institution's environment, (2) collecting data about the institution's performance, (3) analyzing and interpreting the data, and (4) transforming the analyses and interpretations into usable information. Those activities serve not only as a comprehensive source of information about the institution but also as a catalyst for action by others. Not only can the institutional research office provide an objective, institutional, and comprehensive information base for planning and decision making, but it can also give meaning to data and enhance the value of information to users through careful and sensitive presentation.

As Terrass and Pomrenke indicate (1981), the greater the number of decision makers who can be persuaded to work with the researcher towards action, the greater the possibility that institutional and individual needs will be met. This role transition, from reactive to proactive, demands a more perceptive, creative, responsive, and interactive approach to research. An institutional researcher who seeks greater integration with the organization must constantly ask two important questions: what data are most useful to decision makers, and how can I ensure that they will use it?

## Why Is Integration So Important?

What happens when an institutional research function is not successfully integrated into an institution? Most institutional researchers can identify occasions when decision makers ignored volumes of data and pages of narrative and charts. As Norris (1983, p. 168) says, the "finest work of analysis imaginable can be rendered ineffective if it is not presented thoughtfully and in a manner congruent with the needs and preferences of decision makers." A complete, perceptive analysis that does not recognize those "needs and preferences" will be dismissed as useless. It is imperative that analysis begin only after the researcher identifies the audience and the issue or problem the audience seeks to address.

Integrating institutional research is vital to the success of the institution. First, successful integration maximizes the use of information. If the institutional researcher produces accurate, applicable, and statistically sound information but does not bring it to the attention of decision makers in a useful and usable manner, the information has no value: The institutional researcher with information has no power to act on the information, and those who have the power to act do not have the benefit of the information to inform their judgments. Second, introducing information into the layers of the organization focuses decision making on actual knowledge rather than on conventional wisdom. It is quite natural for individuals, despite their limited perspective, to believe that their perceptions and observations about what is happening around them are a sufficient foundation for decision making. The introduction of less biased and value-laden information into the decision-making process can only improve the final outcome. Finally, utilizing institutional research brings to life the multidimensional relationships between information and constituencies and results in improved group discussion and idea generation as well as a broader understanding of the institutional perspective.

## Strategies for Integration

A number of practical and achievable strategies will direct the institutional researcher's work toward greater integration with his or her organization. The importance of each strategy may vary from campus to campus.

**Know Your Institutional Culture.** Terrass and Pomrenke (1981) caution that institutional researchers too often deal with their world as if everyone in it were rational, logical, reasonable, and unbiased. The institutional researcher must develop an awareness of the organizational culture in which he or she lives and learn to function at the social, emotional, and political levels of that organization. They propose a proactive change-agent role for the institutional researcher, "reflecting sensitivity to organizational dynamics and emphasizing strategies for promoting information-based action recommendations" (p. 9). Each institution has its own culture, and different cultures possess very different opinions about what constitutes good and useful information. Politics, group dynamics, staff and faculty relationships, student-life cultures, and the history and traditions of an institution create a unique institutional personality that pervades the actions and interactions of all members of the college community. The wise institutional researcher is one who attends to those patterns of communication, the politics, and the behaviors and values accepted in the organization when considering what kinds of information to produce and how to present the material. If your institutional culture resembles that of IBM, you may want to abandon a casual, informal style of communication and presentation in favor of a more formal one. If you work with artists and designers, you may eschew pages of statistical tables in favor of a few paragraphs of narrative supported by a graph or bar chart. In other words, develop a sensitivity to your cultural norms rather than try to convert your colleagues to your point of view. Schmidtlein (1977) contends that higher education policy makers and information suppliers live in different conceptual worlds and that the former are often inclined to be suspicious of the latter. Your job is to minimize those suspicions by using the language of your institution's culture.

**Know Your Institution's Decision-Making Process.** Mayo and Kallio (1983) assert that decision-making traditions at the organizational level may interfere with information use. Each person or group has its own distinctive style of decision making, which may vary from a data-oriented style to a purely intuitive or political one. Are institutional decisions determined in a formal way? Is the organization collegial or autocratic? What are the formal and informal powers of particular groups? It is important to remember not only the cultural framework for institutional decision making, and who makes the decisions, but also that the results of research will seldom be the sole determinant of the decision (Saupe, 1990). It is also important to remember that decision makers almost always incorporate information from other sources when they make decisions (Hackman, 1989). Knowing your decision makers and knowing how they *believe* they make decisions is crucial to your success in providing information and analysis for them.

**Know Your Audience.** This is a very simple premise. Treat your various audiences as if they were clients and you were their consultant. As a consultant and an analyst you must be prepared to meet the demands of different groups and package information to meet their particular needs and interests. Norris (1983) asserts that the issue of recipients is as important as the purpose and content of the information presented. If you are presenting research results to a faculty committee, think carefully about their perspective on the institution and the points that are most relevant to them. Their time commitment to solving institutional problems may be subordinate to time spent on teaching and professional activities, so tailor your information to address their primary focus as faculty. If you are providing information for senior management, whose primary focus as administrators assumes considerably more attention to institutional problem solving and policy making, your presentation should be more detailed and thorough. Careful attention to each audience's needs increases your credibility as a resource.

**Know the Questions.** As Drucker says (1954, p. 351), "The important and difficult job is never to find the right answer; it is to find the right question." Before you attempt to provide information for any group, get a clear picture of what is being requested. McLaughlin and McLaughlin (1989) outline a few points toward that end by suggesting that the institutional researcher scan the situation and identify potential problems before beginning a project, and identify who wants the information and when it is needed. A most frustrating problem for the institutional researcher exists when the decision makers constantly change the formulation of their questions. Many times those who request information lack a clear idea of what they want to know, let alone what form they want the answer to take. The institutional researcher needs to develop critical investigation skills when attempting to identify the key questions for any group. Not only must the questions be clarified from the start but the clarification process must continue through the life of the project.

**Know the Accepted Channels of Communication.** If you are a diligent memo writer but members of your organization communicate by drifting in and out of each other's offices, then you have misread the organization's accepted channels of communication and you will probably be left out of the critical communication circles. At the very least, you will be viewed as insensitive to the organizational style for communicating and may be ignored by key groups or individuals. Observe closely how the organization communicates internally. Is written communication the honored mode or does everyone casually discuss things in person or on the phone? Is the norm formal presentations or five-minute updates? Do people make decisions during informal meetings or during full staff meetings? Nothing is more important than observing institutional norms and styles as they are manifested in communication behaviors. If you seek greater integration into your organization, pay attention to how ideas travel between constituencies.

**Know Your Place in the Organization.** This may seem obvious, but understanding the consequences of the location of the institutional research function within the organization affects how you interact with campus constituencies and whether they accept or reject your work. The placement of the unit within the organization determines the nature of the institutional researcher's responsibilities. If you report to the finance vice president, a major portion of your work will relate to financial projections and analyses rather than to program evaluation or student-life surveys. Similarly, reporting to the president or senior vice president ensures a broader range of information requests that will impact on policy issues. The institutional research office that reports to a president or senior academic officer is often required to respond to requests more quickly and have greater flexibility in the scheduling of projects, based on priority and last-minute demands. In any case, Ridge (1983) reminds us that the placement of the institutional research office affects its relationships with other offices and should be viewed accordingly when the researcher develops working relationships with various groups. Not only do you reflect your placement in the organization through your interactions, but you develop a style that accommodates the way various groups perceive your usefulness, your purpose, and your power.

**Develop Your People Skills.** If the institutional researcher overlooks the value of good interpersonal skills, all other efforts will be diminished. Patton (1978) cites the critical importance of the positive personal characteristics of the researcher, including an open, approachable, nonthreatening, and not overly technical interpersonal style, combined with informal communication behavior. Regular interactions with subordinates, peers, and supervisors from a variety of professional and academic backgrounds demand a broad range of interpersonal skills that include listening, communicating openly and clearly, clarity of perception, feedback, acknowledgment of group roles and dynamics, team building, problem solving, conflict management, and questioning. Without these skills the role of change agent will remain elusive and the institutional research function will never be completely integrated into the organization (Terrass and Pomrenke, 1981).

**Develop Your Presentation Skills.** Communicating the findings of institutional research is a crucial and challenging task. Effective presentation of research results is the key to linkage with the rest of the organization. All other efforts to integrate will fail if you cannot successfully communicate the information to the decision makers who requested it.

Above all, keep your presentation simple and straightforward. Include only those pieces of information that will state your case effectively. This does not necessarily imply that your presentations should always be brief, although that may often be the case, but it does imply a need for a direct and concise style. Einhorn (1971) asserts that more may not always be better. Although most decision makers and many researchers believe that more information improves decision making, the fact remains that even experienced decision makers use much less information than they assume. Hackman (1989, p. 43) concurs that the judgment of experts and nonexperts does not improve when the pool of information increases. In fact, judgment is sometimes less consistent.

Interpreting the data for your audience is also important. Transform the pages of computer printouts or statistical tables into a readable narrative form. Similarly, always make sure your data are inaccurate, regardless of how much extra time it may take. Nothing will undermine your credibility and undo your hard work faster than inaccurate data.

Whenever possible, use graphs or charts to make your point. Catch the attention of your audience by juxtaposing narrative with pictures to make the presentation interesting. Numerous software packages exist today that will enable you to construct the right combination of narrative and visuals.

Finally, prepare an executive summary for every report. Although you should always prepare a complete report for those who may need or want to see the information in its entirety, an executive summary is an indispensable part of every institutional research report. Furthermore, you should consider packaging portions of your complete report for different audiences, each accompanied by the executive summary. For example, a report on undergraduate enrollment projections may contain graphs depicting growth in the individual majors that will be of interest to appropriate department chairs, while the section of the report that addresses financial implications will be of use to your finance vice-president. Each constituency has its own focus, but as an institutional researcher your first responsibility is to represent the broad institutional implications and perspectives. You link with other groups by directing information to them that you believe they will find most useful and interesting.

**Be a Team Player and Facilitator.** Decision making within the organization is informed and rational to the extent that the institutional researcher can convince decision makers of the value of using vital information. Being a team player involves persuading institutional members that whenever any type of policy issue or planning occurs, the use of carefully prepared information should be part of the process. Working cooperatively with others as part of a team, whether you join the team or form the team, is an essential skill.

**Form Diverse Teams.** This strategy is intricately linked to the previous strategy; the two are interdependent. When you seek the advice and assistance of other constituencies, form work groups that are diverse by mixing your groups horizontally as well as vertically. Obtain or develop the best people to work with you, representing different areas of the organization. Faculty, staff, administrators, trustees, students, and external consultants contribute vastly different perspectives on problems the institution may be facing. Forming teams of individuals who offer different viewpoints makes for more adaptive and creative problem solving.

**Be a Winner.** Adhere to a simple concept: Do not fight losing battles! McLaughlin and McLaughlin (1989) recommend that if the forces at your institution are predisposed against certain types of information or processes, you should look for alternatives. Adopt a positive stance, and resist the temptation to pursue issues that have long since lost their support base or purpose in the organization. Organizations are fluid and dynamic; stay alert to issues that pass in and out of favor, and move with those transitions. As an institutional research office it is imperative to remain politically alert as well as collegial.

**Involve Your Audience from Start to Finish.** Unless your project is very short-lived or easily answered in a sentence or a one-page memo, involve your audience through each phase of the research, no matter how minimally. While you do not want to drown your colleagues in a rush of paper, a brief update or sample outline distributed at various stages of a project will allow them to feel connected and encourage them to add input or make changes along the way. This interchange makes for a better research effort and more usable final results and opens the communication channels between researcher and decision maker. Mystery is not necessary—nor advisable—in the research process. To discuss a project or question with an individual or a group and then to disappear from sight while you work on the answer may do more harm than good when it comes to presenting your results. McLaughlin and McLaughlin (1989, p. 32) phrased it best by saying "involve others by involving them actively in the search for the best possible solutions." Well-timed and succinct communication through the life of a project will ultimately build better relationships with your colleagues.

**Market the Services of the Institutional Research Office.** Market the institutional research function by communicating the availability of your services as well as by reducing the barriers to effective use of information. Not only should you scan the organization to identify gaps between information needs and your resources, but you should also embark on a campaign to educate others about the usefulness of customized research for planning and decision making. A positive attitude about institutional research as an interesting and approachable service is a desirable goal.

One marketing tool is to distribute brief memos to various constituencies reviewing the types of projects you have just completed, along with a note that copies of those reports or summaries are available on request (as appropriate). Sometimes a five- or ten-minute appearance at various staff or faculty meetings to discuss research in progress alerts colleagues to your existence and encourages them to think of you when they are investigating a problem. Greater visibility does not necessarily imply more work for your office, but it may mean more effective use of research and information.

**Establish a Place on Institutional Committees.** This may be easier said than done, and success often depends on your placement in the organization. If it is possible, securing a spot on a few institutional committees will enhance your visibility and allow you to observe directly what is happening within the organization. It is often easier to act on an information request if you have first-hand knowledge of a problem than if you hear about it through a third party. This is not to say that participation on institutional committees will ensure an immediate or comprehensive link to all that is occurring within the organization, but it allows you to get more involved in the operations and deliberations of the institution. The more you know about your environment, the more effectively you can serve it.

## Barriers to Effective Integration

Efforts to coordinate communication, presentation, and interpersonal skills toward successful integration of the institutional research function require supplementary attention to factors that may thwart linkages. McLaughlin and McLaughlin (1989, p. 21) identify many barriers within organizations that "restrain, distract, limit, and bound the effective use of information." The institutional researcher needs to be aware of those limitations and to develop strategies for overcoming them. Some of the possible barriers include:

- Communication gaps between constituencies
- Shifting goals of decision makers
- Interdepartmental competition
- Technology anxiety
- Structural rejection (when institutional research does not support a key person's position on an issue)
- Inappropriate timing
- Mismatch between user needs and analyst perception
- Unethical uses of the institutional researcher's information.

Avoid sabotage of your efforts by watching for some of these pitfalls as you interact with campus groups. Resistance is built into every organization, and awareness is the only means to survival and effectiveness.

## References

Dressel, P. L., and Associates. *Institutional Research in the University: A Handbook.* San Francisco: Jossey-Bass, 1972.

Drucker, P. F. *The Practice of Management.* New York: Harper & Row, 1954.

Einhorn, H. J. "Use of Nonlinear Noncompensatory Models as a Function of Task and Amount of Information." *Organizational Behavior and Performance,* 1971, *6,* 1–27.

Ewell, P. T. "Information for Decision: What's the Use?" In P. T. Ewell (ed.), *Enhancing Information Use in Decision Making.* New Directions for Institutional Research, no. 64. San Francisco: Jossey-Bass, 1989.

Hackman, J. D. "The Psychological Context: Seven Maxims for Institutional Researchers." In P. T. Ewell (ed.), *Enhancing Information Use in Decision Making.* New Directions for Institutional Research, no. 64. San Francisco: Jossey-Bass, 1989.

Maassen, P.A.M. "Institutional Research and Organizational Adaptation." Paper presented at the Eighth European Association for Institutional Research Forum, Loughborough, England, September 3–6, 1986.

McLaughlin, G. W., and McLaughlin, J. S."Barriers to Information Use: The Organizational Context." In P. T. Ewell (ed.), *Enhancing Information Use in Decision Making.* New Directions for Institutional Research, no. 64. San Francisco: Jossey-Bass, 1989.

Mayo, M. H., and Kallio, R. E. "Effective Use of Models in the Decision Process: Theory Grounded in Three Case Studies." In R. R. Perry and J. Y. Reid (eds.), *Institutional Research Issues and Applications 1978–1983*. AIR Professional File 1-16. Tallahassee, Fla.: Association for Institutional Research, 1983.

Norris, D. M. "Triage and the Art of Institutional Research." In R. R. Perry and J. Y. Reid (eds.), *Institutional Research Issues and Applications*. AIR Professional File 1-16. Tallahassee, Fla.: Association for Institutional Research, 1983.

Patton, M. Q. *Utilization-Focused Evaluation*. Newbury Park, Calif.: Sage, 1978.

Peterson, M. W. "Institutional Research: An Evolutionary Perspective." In M. W. Peterson and M. Corcoran (eds.), *Institutional Research in Transition*. New Directions for Institutional Research, no. 46. San Francisco: Jossey-Bass, 1985.

Ridge, J. W. "Organizing for Institutional Research." In R. R. Perry and J. Y. Reid (eds.), *Institutional Research Issues and Applications 1978–1983*. AIR Professional File 1-16. Tallahassee, Fla.: Association for Institutional Research, 1983.

Saupe, J. L. *Functions of Institutional Research*. (2nd ed.) Tallahassee, Fla.: Association for Institutional Research, 1990.

Schmidtlein, F. A. "Information Systems and Concepts of Higher Education Governance." In C. R. Adams (ed.), *Appraising Information Needs of Decision Makers*. New Directions for Institutional Research, no. 15. San Francisco: Jossey-Bass, 1977.

Terrass, S., and Pomrenke, V. "The Institutional Researcher as Change Agent." In J. Lindquist (ed.), *Increasing the Use of Institutional Research*. New Directions for Institutional Research, no. 32. San Francisco: Jossey-Bass, 1981.

*Felice D. Billups is director of institutional research at Rhode Island School of Design.*

*Lenore A. DeLucia is director of institutional research and planning at Rhode Island College.*

*While each institutional research office has its own unique style and mission, the commonalities shared by such offices lead to some useful prescriptions for establishing effective units.*

# Putting the Building Blocks into Place for Effective Institutional Research

*Jennifer B. Presley*

The theme for the thirtieth annual Association for Institutional Research (AIR) Forum was "Institutional Research—Coming of Age." The coming of age of the profession is multifaceted. Institutional research is a growing enterprise, spurred on by demands for institutional accountability and outcomes assessment; it is becoming a more sophisticated enterprise, through wide access to computing tools that did not exist even five years ago; it is a maturing enterprise, with well-established offices in major research institutions experiencing "elaborate profusion" and the concomitant challenges that accompany the proliferation of expertise throughout an institution. These diverse movements toward maturity do not lead to homogeneity but to increased variety within the profession, especially variety of organizational arrangements for accomplishing institutional research and of the individual tasks and scope of responsibilities of institutional researchers themselves.

Volkwein, in Chapter One, proposed a useful framework for considering the variety of organizational structures and associated tasks that encompass institutional research. Under this typology there are four arrangements: the craft structure, typified by the one-person office in a small institution; the small adhocracy of two to three staff with wide variance in the skills in and responsibilities of the office; the professional bureaucracy, represented by offices of at least four staff and a degree of internal hierarchy; and finally, *elaborate profusion,* where activities and expertise proliferate throughout the (usually large, research) institution. The majority of institutional research offices in Volkwein's study of the North East Association for Institutional Research membership are best described as craft structures. About one quarter were small adhocracies, typically in institutions with enrollments between 5,000 and 10,000. The professional bureaucracy, while perhaps what we consider to be the "typical" office of institutional research, in fact existed in less than 20 percent of the institutions. A few institutions exhibited "elaborate profusion." There seems to be a strong relationship between the type of institution (size and mission) and the type of institutional research function that best serves its needs. Thus, we should not expect a maturing process to be occurring within the profession whereby we would expect over time to see a significant shift from the dominance of craft structures to professional bureaucracies or elaborate profusion.

On the other hand, several chapters in the volume postulate the need for offices to acquire a range of experts as they strive to become more effective. The scope of research outlined by Middaugh in Chapter Two cannot be accomplished within a craft structure. Institutional expectations must be realistic for the one-person office. In Chapter Three, Wilton describes a typical data environment facing the new institutional research office. Her discussion highlights the enormous effort that must lie behind the development of a data resource for institutional analysis. Miselis, in Chapter Five, lays out an important strategy for tethering data anarchy but strongly recommends the appointment of at least a data administrator to accomplish this task. Tetlow, in Chapter Six, emphasizes the importance of having staff within the institutional research office who are competent in the technical aspects of computing. Both Taylor, in Chapter Two, and Nichols and Wolff in Chapter Seven note the disparity between the background of many institutional researchers and the skills needed to establish an effective assessment capacity. These responsibilities cannot be confronted single-handedly.

Many of the authors emphasize the importance of the "first-order" mission of institutional research best described by Tetlow when he says that "data must still be collected, purified of errors and anomalies, and standardized so that aberrations are properly revealed" (Chapter Six). The institutional researcher in the one-person office can only hope to address second-order tasks such as assessment and policy analysis by creating teams of helpers throughout the institution, from the registrar to computing support personnel to the faculty themselves. At the other end of the spectrum, for the institutional researcher in a large, complex institution that is experiencing "elaborate profusion," the establishment of a full-fledged institutionwide information resource management strategy, as described by Miselis in Chapter Five, becomes critical to success. And for those who find themselves somewhere in the middle, an appropriate combination of strategies must be woven to build the support structures necessary for effective institutional research.

## Establishing Effective Institutional Research Offices

Each of the chapters in this volume provides practical strategies for addressing components of the task of establishing an effective institutional research office. Here I summarize the major precepts that are of importance for effective institutional research (with the relevant chapters given in parentheses).

• Offices must be placed high enough in the organizational structure for the staff to be aware of the major issues and decisions facing senior management. This enables them to anticipate management needs for information and to respond appropriately and quickly. While location will depend on the structure of the specific institution, there are some general guidelines. In small institutions, location within the office of the chief executive officer is advisable. In larger institutions, reporting to the vice-president for academic affairs can be a satisfactory alternative (Chapter Two). When assessment responsibilities are to include both academic and administrative functions, location within the office of the CEO is appropriate, independent of the size of the institution (Chapter Seven).

• The first-order responsibilities of institutional research—data collection, purification, and reporting—must receive ongoing attention and form the base on which second-order studies—policy analysis, assessment, and planning—are built (Chapters One, Four, Six, and Seven).

• New offices of institutional research will take some time to establish a first-order level of activity that facilitates routine reporting and analysis (Chapters Four and Seven). It is essential to set reasonable expectations for productivity. One-person offices may always find it difficult to accomplish more than first-order tasks (Chapter One).

• When establishing an institutional research capacity it is important to understand the specific needs of the institution. Understanding the particular culture of the campus will facilitate communication of results (Chapter Eight). Knowing why the office is being established will help in setting priorities. Meeting these initial needs early on will bring long-lasting credibility to the unit.

• Lead institutional researchers are usually generalists. They must have solid quantitative skills, often gained through social science study at the graduate level (Chapters One and Two), excellent oral and written presentation skills, and outstanding communication skills (Chapter Eight).

• Offices also need specialists. As more computing power is placed on the desk top, offices will need their own computing expert if they are to maximize their use of this new technology (Chapter Six). Bringing the management of institutional data under control requires the expertise of a data administrator (Chapter Five). Assessment activities require expertise in measurement, testing, and survey research, skills that the present-day institutional researcher may not have (Chapter Seven). It is unreasonable to expect all of these attributes to be found in one person.

• It is important to build on what already exists within the organization. Tap into the current computing capacity on campus and assess the extent to which it can meet immediate needs (Chapter Four). Is anyone on campus already doing analysis and reporting? Avoid duplication of effort wherever possible.

• A significant amount of initial effort will be spent on marshalling the resources needed for effective institutional research. While it makes sense to start by taking advantage of existing circumstances, acquiring adequate computing independence and staff to accomplish your mission should be the long-term goal (Chapter Six). Look to opportunities beyond the institution—the state board may have a little money to help acquire computing tools, or another unit may be able to help in exchange for services.

## Institutional Research as a Professional Enterprise

The major purpose of this volume has been to provide suggestions for those faced with establishing an institutional research enterprise. No matter the size of the enterprise, much time and effort will be devoted initially to obtaining essential resources—hardware, software, and staff—and establishing reliable data for reporting and analysis. Others facing this task have found that at least a year is needed to set the unit on its course. I hope, however, that the role of the institutional researcher will not stop there. Billups and DeLucia, in Chapter Eight, give us ideas for taking our responsibilities further and becoming activists. No matter how small the enterprise, the institutional researcher can follow many of their suggestions. When institutional research is perceived simply as a number-crunching activity, not only does the profession lose, but so does each and every institution where this attitude prevails. Even if limited staffing prevents an office from undertaking major second-order activities, it is possible to turn first-order reporting into an interesting and important activity. I have an operating rule in my office not to simply provide numbers in response to a question but to understand the question being asked, to reinterpret it when necessary, and to provide a context for the answer. Institutions that have not had the luxury of experiencing the usefulness of competent institutional research need to be taught how to take advantage of the new enterprise, and institutional researchers themselves are in the best position to accomplish this.

The strategies outlined in this volume have been learned from many years' experience in the field, and we hope that they together will help guide the way for our fellow institutional researchers as they strive to establish effective institutional research offices.

*Jennifer B. Presley is executive director of the office of policy research and planning, University of Massachusetts at Boston.*

# Index

# ORDERING INFORMATION

NEW DIRECTIONS FOR INSTITUTIONAL RESEARCH is a series of paperback books that provides planners and administrators in all types of academic institutions with guidelines in such areas as resource coordination, information analysis, program evaluation, and institutional management. Books in the series are published quarterly in Fall, Winter, Spring, and Summer and are available for purchase by subscription as well as by single copy.

SUBSCRIPTIONS for 1990 cost $42.00 for individuals (a savings of 20 percent over single-copy prices) and $56.00 for institutions, agencies, and libraries. Please do not send institutional checks for personal subscriptions. Standing orders are accepted.

SINGLE COPIES cost $12.95 when payment accompanies order. (California, New Jersey, New York, and Washington, D.C., residents please include appropriate sales tax.) Billed orders will be charged postage and handling.

DISCOUNTS FOR QUANTITY ORDERS are available. Please write to the address below for information.

ALL ORDERS must include either the name of an individual or an official purchase order number. Please submit your order as follows:

*Subscriptions:* specify series and year subscription is to begin
*Single copies:* include individual title code (such as IR1)

*MAIL ALL ORDERS TO:*
*Jossey-Bass Inc., Publishers*
*350 Sansome Street*
*San Francisco, California 94104*

OTHER TITLES AVAILABLE IN THE
NEW DIRECTIONS FOR INSTITUTIONAL RESEARCH SERIES
*Patrick T. Terenzini* Editor-in-Chief
*Ellen Earle Chaffee,* Associate Editor

IR65 The Effect of Assessment on Minority Student Participation, *Michael T. Nettles*
IR64 Enhancing Information Use in Decision Making, *Peter T. Ewell*
IR63 Managing Faculty Resources, *G. Gregory Lozier, Michael J. Dooris*
IR62 Studying the Impact of Student Aid on Institutions, *Robert H. Fenske*
IR61 Planning and Managing Higher Education Facilities, *Harvey H. Kaiser*
IR60 Alumni Research: Methods and Applications, *Gerlinda S. Melchiori*
IR59 Implementing Outcomes Assessment: Promise and Perils, *Trudy W. Banta*
IR58 Applying Statistics in Institutional Research, *Bernard D. Yancey*
IR57 Improving Teaching and Learning Through Research, *Joan S. Stark, Lisa A. Mets*
IR56 Evaluating Administrative Services and Programs, *Jon F. Wergin, Larry A. Braskamp*
IR55 Managing Information in Higher Education, *E. Michael Staman*
IR54 Designing and Using Market Research, *Robert S. Lay, Jean J. Endo*
IR53 Conducting Interinstitutional Comparisons, *Paul T. Brinkman*
IR52 Environmental Scanning for Strategic Leadership, *Patrick M. Callan*
IR51 Enhancing the Management of Fund Raising, *John A. Dunn, Jr.*
IR50 Measuring Faculty Research Performance, *John W. Creswell*
IR49 Applying Decision Support Systems in Higher Education, *John Rohrbaugh, Anne Taylor McCartt*
IR47 Assessing Educational Outcomes, *Peter T. Ewell*
IR39 Applying Methods and Techniques of Futures Research, *James L. Morrison, William L. Renfro, Wayne I. Boucher*
IR37 Using Research for Strategic Planning, *Norman P. Uhl*
IR36 Studying Student Attrition, *Ernest T. Pascarella*
IR35 Information Technology: Innovations and Applications, *Bernard Sheehan*
IR34 Qualitative Methods for Institutional Research, *Eileen Kuhns, S. V. Martorana*
IR33 Effective Planned Change Strategies, *G. Melvin Hipps*
IR32 Increasing the Use of Institutional Research, *Jack Lindquist*
IR31 Evaluation of Management and Planning Systems, *Nick L. Poulton*

## From the Editor

This volume of *New Directions for Institutional Research* is designed to assist both those who are establishing an institutional research function for the first time and those who are invigorating an existing unit. The authors write from their own experiences as institutional researchers involved with development activities. They provide guidelines for how to approach tasks and avoid major pitfalls. Seasoned institutional researchers will find that many of the chapters provide a useful update on such issues as computing tools, data administration, the establishment of an assessment capacity, and interpersonal communications.